Compatibility Modeling

Data and Knowledge Applications
for Clothing Matching

Synthesis Lectures on Information Concepts, Retrieval, and Services

Editor
Gary Marchionini, *University of North Carolina, Chapel Hill*

Synthesis Lectures on Information Concepts, Retrieval, and Services publishes short books on topics pertaining to information science and applications of technology to information discovery, production, distribution, and management. Potential topics include: data models, indexing theory and algorithms, classification, information architecture, information economics, privacy and identity, scholarly communication, bibliometrics and webometrics, personal information management, human information behavior, digital libraries, archives and preservation, cultural informatics, information retrieval evaluation, data fusion, relevance feedback, recommendation systems, question answering, natural language processing for retrieval, text summarization, multimedia retrieval, multilingual retrieval, and exploratory search.

Compatibility Modeling: Data and Knowledge Applications for Clothing Matching
Xuemeng Song, Liqiang Nie, and Yinglong Wang

ISBN: 978-3-031-01193-1   paperback
ISBN: 978-3-031-02321-7   ebook
ISBN: 978-3-031-00228-1   hardcover

DOI 10.1007/978-3-031-02321-7

A Publication in the Springer series
SYNTHESIS LECTURES ON INFORMATION CONCEPTS, RETRIEVAL, AND SERVICES

Lecture #69
Series Editor: Gary Marchionini, *University of North Carolina, Chapel Hill*
Series ISSN
Print 1947-945X   Electronic 1947-9468

Compatibility Modeling

Data and Knowledge Applications
for Clothing Matching

Xuemeng Song
Shandong University

Liqiang Nie
Shandong University

Yinglong Wang
Qilu University of Technology (Shandong Academic of Science)

SYNTHESIS LECTURES ON INFORMATION CONCEPTS, RETRIEVAL, AND SERVICES #69

ABSTRACT

Nowadays, fashion has become an essential aspect of people's daily life. As each outfit usually comprises several complementary items, such as a top, bottom, shoes, and accessories, a proper outfit largely relies on the harmonious matching of these items. Nevertheless, not everyone is good at outfit composition, especially those who have a poor fashion aesthetic. Fortunately, in recent years the number of online fashion-oriented communities, like IQON and Chictopia, as well as e-commerce sites, like Amazon and eBay, has grown. The tremendous amount of real-world data regarding people's various fashion behaviors has opened a door to automatic clothing matching.

Despite its significant value, compatibility modeling for clothing matching that assesses the compatibility score for a given set of (equal or more than two) fashion items, e.g., a blouse and a skirt, yields tough challenges: (a) the absence of comprehensive benchmark; (b) comprehensive compatibility modeling with the multi-modal feature variables is largely untapped; (c) how to utilize the domain knowledge to guide the machine learning; (d) how to enhance the interpretability of the compatibility modeling; and (e) how to model the user factor in the personalized compatibility modeling. These challenges have been largely unexplored to date.

In this book, we shed light on several state-of-the-art theories on compatibility modeling. In particular, to facilitate the research, we first build three large-scale benchmark datasets from different online fashion websites, including IQON and Amazon. We then introduce a general data-driven compatibility modeling scheme based on advanced neural networks. To make use of the abundant fashion domain knowledge, i.e., clothing matching rules, we next present a novel knowledge-guided compatibility modeling framework. Thereafter, to enhance the model interpretability, we put forward a prototype-wise interpretable compatibility modeling approach. Following that, noticing the subjective aesthetics of users, we extend the general compatibility modeling to the personalized version. Moreover, we further study the real-world problem of personalized capsule wardrobe creation, aiming to generate a minimum collection of garments that is both compatible and suitable for the user. Finally, we conclude the book and present future research directions, such as the generative compatibility modeling, virtual try-on with arbitrary poses, and clothing generation.

KEYWORDS

compatibility modeling, clothing matching, interpretable modeling, knowledge distillation, preference modeling, personalized capsule wardrobe

Contents

Preface

Undoubtedly, clothing plays an essential role in people's daily life, as a proper outfit can greatly empower one's favorable impression. As each outfit usually involves multiple complementary items, such as top, bottom, shoes, and accessories, to a great extent, the key to a proper outfit lies in harmonious clothing matching. However, not everyone is a natural-born fashion stylist, which makes choosing compatible clothes a tedious and even annoying daily routine. It thus deserves our attention to develop an effective clothing matching scheme to help people find the suitable match for a given item and make a proper outfit. Thanks to the proliferation of online fashion-oriented communities, such as IQON and Chictopia, as well as e-commerce sites, such as Amazon and eBay, where a tremendous amount of rich real-world data regarding users' shopping, reviewing, and coordinating behaviors on fashion items have been accumulated, researchers are able to investigate the code in clothing matching.

In a sense, the problem of clothing matching posed here primarily requires modeling the human notion of the compatibility between fashion items. Despite its significant value, compatibility modeling for clothing matching that involves not only a large number of feature variables but also complicated factors such as the domain knowledge and user factor, suffers from the following tough challenges:

(a) Absence of comprehensive benchmark. How can we construct comprehensive datasets to facilitate the validation of compatibility models?

(b) Comprehensive modeling. Existing studies mainly focused on measuring the compatibility based on visual images of items but failed to take their contextual information into account. Accordingly, the comprehensive compatibility modeling with multi-modal feature variables is largely untapped.

(c) Knowledge incorporation. As an integral part of people's daily life, clothing matching domain has accumulated valuable knowledge. How to utilize domain knowledge to guide machine learning is another challenge we are facing.

(d) Interpretability enhancement. A realistic compatibility modeling scheme should not only give the final decision on whether the given fashion items are compatible or not, but also provide the underlying reasons. How to enhance the interpretability of the compatibility modeling constitutes a crucial challenge; and

(e) User factor. The user aesthetics on clothing matching can be subjective due to their different fashion tastes. Meanwhile, user body shapes also affect the compatibility modeling for clothing matching to a certain extent. Thereby, personalized compatibility modeling should be investigated.

Besides these, several other challenges have been raised, including confidence assignment of various knowledge rules for clothing matching, user preference modeling, and user body shape modeling in compatibility modeling.

In fact, the huge economic value of the fashion industry has drawn great attention from many researchers. Existing efforts mainly focus on tackling the problem of clothing retrieval, clothing recommendation, and fashionability prediction. However, only a limited number of studies have been dedicated to the compatibility modeling, not to mention the knowledge-guided and personalized compatibility modeling, aspects. Noticing this timely opportunity, we present in this book some state-of-the-art theories on compatibility modeling. In particular, we first summarize the method of building several comprehensive benchmark datasets, which have been released to facilitate other researchers. We then introduce how to model the general compatibility that can be affected by complicated factors in a pure data-driven manner. To further boost performance, we next present a novel knowledge-guided compatibility modeling framework, where a knowledge-encoding method is introduced. Thereafter, we enhance the interpretability of the compatibility modeling scheme with the latent compatible/incompatible prototype learning. Following that, we extend the general compatibility modeling to a personalized one, based on which we further study the real-world application of personalized capsule wardrobe creation. Finally, we conclude the book and present the future research directions in the compatibility modeling domain, such as generative compatibility modeling, virtual try-on with arbitrary poses, and clothing generation.

This book presents preliminary research on fashion compatibility modeling, and we expect it can evoke active researchers to work on this exciting area. Overall, this book presents an in-depth introduction to the compatibility modeling problem, by shedding light on the important research topics and the latest developments in the field. It is suitable for students, researchers, and practitioners who are interested in the compatibility modeling for clothing matching task. Notably, although the datasets used in this work may be biased to the female on account that male users are not as active in online fashion-oriented websites, the theories presented in this book can be effortlessly applied to male clothing as long as the corresponding data are available. If in this book we have been able to dream further than others have, it is because we are standing on the shoulders of giants.

Xuemeng Song, Liqiang Nie, and Yinglong Wang
September 2019

Acknowledgments

This book would not have been completed, or at least not be what it looks like now, without the support of many colleagues, especially those from the iLearn Center in Shandong University. It is a pleasure to take this opportunity to acknowledge them for their contributions to this time-consuming book project.

Our first and foremost thanks undoubtedly go to colleagues who are also the contributors of some chapters of this book: Dr. Fuli Feng at National University of Singapore, Miss. Xianjing Han, Miss. Jinhuan Liu, Miss. Xue Dong, and Mr. Xin Yang at iLearn Center in Shandong University. Thanks for their active participation in the technical discussion of this book and their constructive feedback and comments that have been significantly helpful in shaping this book.

Second, we would like to express our heartfelt gratitude to Miss. Qian Liu and Miss. Xiaoli Li, who spared no effort in polishing the earlier drafts.

Third, we are very grateful to the anonymous reviewer. Despite his/her busy schedule, the reviewer read the book very carefully and gave us many insightful and constructive suggestions, making the book more readable.

Fourth, we sincerely extend our thanks to Morgan & Claypool and particularly the editor, Dr. Gary Marchionini, and the Executive Editor, Ms. Diane Cerra, for their valuable suggestions on this book. They also helped to make the book publishing process smooth and enjoyable.

Last, our thanks are reserved to our beloved families for their selfless consideration, endless love, and unconditional support.

Xuemeng Song, Liqiang Nie, and Yinglong Wang
September 2019

CHAPTER 1

Introduction

1.1 BACKGROUND

According to the FashionUnited.com,[1] the global fashion and apparel industry has been valued at three trillion dollars, making up 2% of the world's gross domestic product, demonstrating the blossoming of the fashion market and people's great demand for clothing. In fact, apart from the physiological needs, people also have reasons of self esteem for clothes, as dressing properly is seen as an important part of daily life. As each outfit usually involves multiple complementary items (e.g., tops, bottoms, and shoes), the key to a proper outfit usually lies in harmonious clothing matching. Nevertheless, the tremendous amount of fashion items available tends to overwhelm people, making it rather difficult for them to compose suitable outfits, especially for those who lack a good fashion aesthetic. It is thus highly desirable to devise an automatic clothing matching scheme to help people find a suitable match for a given item in order to make a harmonious outfit.

Meanwhile, recent years have witnessed the proliferation of various online fashion-oriented communities, such as Polyvore,[2] IQON,[3] and Chictopia,[4] where fashion experts can share their fashion tips by showcasing their outfit compositions to the public. Figure 1.1 shows several composition examples on Polyvore. As a matter of fact, for better illustration, clothing items on fashion-oriented communities are usually associated with not only visual images with clean backgrounds but also rich contextual metadata, such as titles and categories. Accordingly, the tremendous volume of outfit compositions with rich metadata naturally makes the online fashion-oriented community a wonderful venue to investigate the code in clothing matching. In addition to these fashion-oriented communities, popular e-commerce websites, like Amazon[5] and eBay[6] that enable users to review their purchased products with detailed size descriptions, also provide significant cues for clothing matching. These valuable reviews can not only tell users' preferences on fashion items but also their body shapes, which would facilitate the personalized clothing matching.

---

[1]https://fashionunited.com/global-fashion-industry-statistics/

[2]Polyvore has been acquired by the global fashion platform Ssense in 2018. Previously, fashion lovers could share their outfits compositions to the public on Polyvore.

[3]http://www.iqon.jp/

[4]http://www.chictopia.com/

[5]https://www.amazon.com/

[6]https://www.ebay.com/

| (a) Composition 1. | (b) Composition 2. | (c) Composition 3. |

Figure 1.1: Example outfit compositions on Polyvore.

1.2   CHALLENGES

In this work, we focus on the essential problem for clothing matching: compatibility modeling, which aims to assess the compatibility score for a given set of (equal or more than two) fashion items, e.g., a T-shirt and jeans. As the compatibility modeling involves not only a large number of feature variables but also complicated factors such as the domain knowledge and user factor, it suffers from the following challenges.

First is the comprehensive modeling. Existing studies have mainly focused on measuring the compatibility between fashion items based on their visual images but ignored the contextual information, such as the item description title and categories, which can also convey the key features of items and contribute to the compatibility modeling. Moreover, as different modalities characterize the same fashion item, they should preserve certain semantic correlations. Accordingly, how to model the coherent correlation between the visual and contextual modalities of the same fashion item, and seamlessly fuse different modality data to boost the performance, is a major challenge we are facing.

Second is the knowledge incorporation. In fact, as an essential aspect of people's daily life, much valuable knowledge (e.g., the clothing matching rules) in the fashion domain has been accumulated, which may guide the pure data-driven compatibility modeling scheme to learn better. Nevertheless, the human knowledge in the fashion domain is usually implicitly conveyed by the large amount of outfits composed by fashion experts, and tends to be unstructured and fuzzy, making it intractable to directly embed the knowledge into the data-driven learning scheme. Therefore, how to properly encode the domain knowledge, integrate it into the pure data-driven learning scheme, and hence enable the model to learn from both the specific data and the knowledge rules pose another challenge for us.

Third is the model interpretability. To comprehensively fulfill the clothing matching task, the compatibility modeling scheme should not only give the final decision on whether or not the given fashion items are compatible, but also interpret the discordance of incompatible outfits. Nevertheless, most existing studies focus more on employing deep learning methods to learn effective representations for fashion items, and hence suffer from the poor interpretability, making them less useful in practice. Accordingly, how to enhance the interpretability of the compatibility modeling scheme proves difficult.

Fourth is the user factor. In reality, different people may have different fashion tastes, and their aesthetics can be rather subjective. For example, given a T-shirt, some people prefer jeans to make an outfit, while others may like skirts. Additionally, people with different body shapes tend to go with different types of fashion items, to highlight their figure strengths and weaken the shortcomings. Consequently, how to incorporate the user factor, such as personal preference and body shape, in the traditional item-based compatibility modeling framework, making the matching results not only of high compatibility from the general item-item perspective but also cater for user taste as well as body shape from the personal item-user angle, contributes a crucial challenge.

The last challenge is the absence of a comprehensive benchmark. In fact, several fashion datasets have been collected in existing studies, for example, the *WoW* [76], *Exact Street2Shop* [29], and *Fashion-136K* [49]. However, most existing released datasets mainly include the visual metadata of fashion items but lack the contextual description, as aforementioned, which also comprises a great deal of valuable information on items. In addition, the user context is usually absent from most existing released datasets in the fashion domain, which hinders the research on integrating the user factor into the compatibility modeling. Therefore, it is necessary to construct comprehensive benchmark datasets to fulfill the validation of compatibility models.

Furthermore, several other issues come into being, such as the confidence of various knowledge rules in the guidance of compatibility modeling, user preference modeling, and user body shape factor in compatibility modeling, which increase the challenge of the proposed problem.

1.3   OUR SOLUTIONS

To address the aforementioned research challenges, we present several state-of-the-art compatibility modeling theories and verify them in different contexts, ranging from the general compatibility modeling, personalized compatibility modeling to personalized wardrobe creation.

To facilitate the evaluation of our proposed schemes, we first created three large-scale real-world datasets from several online fashion-oriented communities for the above three tasks, respectively. In particular, Dataset I is created by collecting the outfit compositions of fashion experts on Polyvore. Considering that it lacks enough user context, we build Dataset II by crawling the historical outfits of 6,191 users from IQON. Then to incorporate the user's figure/body shape and create suitable user wardrobe, we build Dataset III comprising purchase histories of

11,784 users on Amazon. The underlying philosophy is that, in a sense, the user body shape can be derived from the sizes of his/her purchased fashion items.

For the general compatibility modeling, we first introduce a data-driven compatibility modeling scheme with neural networks, where both modalities of fashion items are exploited. The core is to find the latent compatibility space which can bridge the gap between complementary fashion items from heterogeneous spaces and facilitate the compatibility measurement between items. Toward this end, we resort to the advanced neural networks to capture the subtle compatibility factors, like color, material, and pattern. Finally, the Bayesian Personalized Ranking (BPR) framework is adopted to exploit the implicit pairwise preference between complementary fashion items.

In fact, as an essential aspect of people's life, the fashion domain has accumulated rich human knowledge on clothing matching. To boost the performance, we then present a novel knowledge-guided compatibility modeling framework, which is able to learn the latent compatibility space from not only the specific data samples but also the general domain knowledge. In particular we adopt the teacher-student scheme, where the teacher network can guide the student data-driven learning network with the domain knowledge, namely, the clothing matching rules. Considering that different knowledge rules may have different confidence in guiding different sample pairs, we employ the attention mechanism to adaptively assign the rule confidence.

To enhance the model explainability, we devise a prototype-wise interpretable compatibility modeling scheme, based on the key assumption that compatible fashion items tend to follow certain underlying harmonious attribute interaction prototypes, while the incompatible ones would like to share some unfavorable prototypes. The proposed scheme seamlessly unifies the compatibility modeling and latent prototype learning, where the non-negative matrix factorization technique is employed to discover the latent prototypes. The learned prototypes can be regarded as the templates to interpret the discordant attribute and suggest the alternative ones.

To deal with the user factor in compatibility assessment, we then propose a personalized compatibility modeling scheme between fashion items with the user factor taken into account. In particular, the proposed scheme consists of two essential components: general compatibility modeling and personal preference modeling. In particular, apart from the traditional item-item interaction, user-item interaction (i.e., the user's preferences on fashion items) is captured with the matrix factorization framework. To comprehensively model the user preference, the latent preference factors on both modalities of fashion items are introduced.

As mentioned previously, user body shapes can also affect the compatibility modeling in a sense. People with different body shapes would go with different types of clothing items. Meanwhile, each outfit usually involves more than two pieces of fashion items. Toward this end, we further present a combinatorial optimization-based personalized compatibility modeling paradigm for outfits with the real-world application of personalized capsule wardrobe creation. Both the user modeling, including the user preference and user body shape modeling, and garment modeling are jointly explored.

1.4   BOOK STRUCTURE

The remainder of this book consists of six chapters. Chapter 2 introduces the data collection, where three datasets are created for the evaluation of the proposed schemes. Chapter 3 presents a general data-driven scheme for the compatibility modeling in the clothing matching context. In Chapter 4, we propose a novel knowledge-guided compatibility modeling model that incorporates the rich fashion domain knowledge to boost the performance. In Chapter 5, we introduce a prototype-guided interpretable compatibility modeling framework which aims to generate explanations for the compatibility evaluation and enhance the model interpretability with the latent prototype learning. In Chapter 6, we study the personalized compatibility modeling between fashion items by incorporating the user factor (i.e., the user preference) in clothing matching. In Chapter 7, we further explore the personalized compatibility modeling for outfits with the real-world application of personalized wardrobe creation, where the user's body shape is taken into account. We conclude this book and discuss future research directions in Chapter 8.

CHAPTER 2

Data Collection

In this chapter, we introduce the three datasets we collected, corresponding to the tasks of the general compatibility modeling, personalized compatibility modeling, and personal wardrobe creation, respectively.

2.1 DATASET I FOR GENERAL COMPATIBILITY MODELING

In fact, several fashion datasets have been collected for different research purposes, for instance, the *WoW* [76], *Exact Street2Shop* [29], and *Fashion-136K* [49]. However, most of the existing released datasets are collected from wild street photos and thus inevitably involve a clothing parsing technique, which still remains a great challenge in the computer vision domain [125, 126]. In addition, these datasets lack the rich contextual metadata of each fashion item, which makes it difficult to fully model the fashion items. Therefore, to guarantee the evaluation quality and facilitate the experiment conduction, we constructed our own dataset **FashionVC** by crawling outfits created by fashion experts on Polyvore. In particular, we first collected a seed set of popular outfits on Polyvore, based on which we tracked 248 fashion experts. We then crawled the historical outfits published by them, based on which we constructed the ground truth for positive item pairs. Considering that certain improper outfits can be accidentally created by users on Polyvore, we also set a threshold $z = 50$ with respect to the number of "likes" for each outfit to ensure the quality of the positive fashion pairs. Finally, we obtained 20,726 outfits with 14,871 tops and 13,663 bottoms. For each fashion item, we particularly collected its visual image, categories, and title description.

Table 2.1 lists several examples of fashion items in our dataset. Each fashion item is associated with an image, a title, and several categories in terms of different granularity.

2.2 DATASET II FOR PERSONALIZED COMPATIBILITY MODELING

As a matter of fact, most of the existing publicly available datasets lack the user context, which makes it intractable to tackle the personalized clothing matching problem. It is worth noting that although the dataset *Amazon* [86] contains the valuable user contexts but it focuses more on the item recommendation based on the user preference and hence lacks the ground truth regarding the coordination among fashion items. Moreover, the dataset used in [43] contains

Table 2.1: Fashion item examples. "− >" indicates the category hierarchy.

ID	Image	Category	Title
1		Women's Fashion -> Clothing ->Tops	River Island Resort Light Blue Denim Halter Neck Top
2		Women's Fashion -> Clothing ->Skirts -> Mini Skirts	Plaid Ruffled Mini Skirt
3		Women's Fashion -> Jeans -> Flared Jeans	MiH Jeans Mid-rise Stretch-velvet Flares Jeans

only 150 users, which hinders the practical evaluation. Therefore, to bridge this gap, we created a new large dataset for personalized clothing matching. In particular, we crawled our data from the popular fashion web service IQON, where users are encouraged to create outfits by coordinating fashion items from complementary categories (e.g., tops, bottoms, shoes, and accessories).

In particular, we first collected a set of popular outfits on IQON as the seeds, and by tracking them, we obtained 6,191 users. Thereafter, we crawled the latest 500 historical outfits of each user due to the following twofold concerns: (1) extremely active users have created thousands of outfits, where according to our pilot study, the most active user has 4,562 outfits, which would result in the imbalanced dataset and (2) users' tastes on clothing matching may shift gradually and it thus should be more reasonable to be reflected by their latest outfits. To ensure the quality of the dataset, we filtered out the users with less than 5 historical outfits and only retained the items belonging to the six common categories: *Coat, Top, Bottom, One Piece,*[1] *Shoes,* and *Accessories*. Thereafter, we obtained 308,747 outfits created by 3,568 users with 672,335 fashion items. The statistics of the dataset is listed in Table 2.2. For each fashion item, we particularly crawled its profile, including the visual image, categories, attributes, and item description, as shown in Figure 2.1.

---

[1]One piece refers to the dress and tunic.

Table 2.2: The number of items of each category

Category	Number	Category	Number
Outerwear	35,765	Top	119,895
Bottom	77,813	Shoes	106.598
One Piece	25,816	Accessories	306,448

Figure 2.1: Screenshot of the item profile in IQON. We particularly collected the information highlighted by the purple boxes. It is worth noting that the text has been translated here for illustration.

2.3 DATASET III FOR PERSONALIZED WARDROBE CREATION

In reality, it is hard to collect a comprehensive dataset that can well support the personalized capsule wardrobe creation considering both the user modeling and garment modeling. Therefore, in this work, we employ different datasets in the user modeling and garment modeling. Polyvore dataset [31], comprising 21,889 outfits with 164,379 fashion items involving corresponding image and description, is adopted for the garment modeling.

As for the user modeling, although McAuley et al. [87] has introduced a public large-scale Amazon dataset for personalized fashion recommendation tasks, it fails to incorporate the user body shape-related data, which makes the dataset unsuitable for our comprehensive PCW creation. Fortunately, we noticed that the user purchase history, especially the size of purchased fashion items, involving specific body measurements (such as the hip girth and waist girth), conveys more reliable cues of the user body shape. Inspired by this, we constructed our own dataset, named bodyFashion, by collecting user purchase histories from Amazon. In particular, we first collected a set of popular fashion items from Amazon. After that, based on item comments, we tracked a lot of Amazon users. We crawled their recent historical purchase records (limited by 100 records), and selected the fashion items from them. In order to guarantee the quality of the dataset for PCW creation, we screened out users with less than 6 historical purchase records, and then obtained 116,528 user-item records involving 11,784 users and 75,695 fashion items. Each item comprises its image, title, and category metadata. Both purchase sizes and ratings are available for each user-item record. A record example is illustrated in Figure 2.2.

Figure 2.2: An example of bodyFashion. Users are associated with rich labeled fashion items they purchased.

2.4   SUMMARY

In this chapter, we introduce three real-world datasets collected from the fashion-oriented online communities: Polyvore, Iqon, and Amazon, respectively. In particular, Dataset I consisting of 20,726 outfits with 14,871 tops and 13,663 bottoms is collected for the general compatibility modeling, while Dataset II comprising 308,747 outfits created by 3,568 users with 672,335 fashion items is created for the personalized compatibility modeling. In addition, we build Dataset III to testify the effectiveness of our model in the real-world application of personalized wardrobe creation. We have released all these datasets to facilitate other researchers in the community of fashion compatibility modeling.

CHAPTER 3

Data-Driven Compatibility Modeling

3.1 INTRODUCTION

In this chapter, we aim to investigate the practical problem of clothing matching, without loss of generality, by particularly answering the question "which bottom matches the given top." The problem we pose here primarily requires modeling human notion of the compatibility between fashion items. However, modeling such subtle notion regarding compatibility is non-trivial due to the following challenges. First, the compatibility between fashion items usually involves color, material, pattern, shape, and other design factors. In addition, human notion of compatibility is not absolute but relative, as people can only tell that a pair of items is more suitable to each other than other items. Therefore, how to accurately measure the compatibility between items constitutes a tough challenge. Second, existing studies mainly focus on measuring the compatibility based on images of items but fail to take the contextual information of fashion items into consideration. As a matter of fact, similar to visual images, contextual descriptions also present the key features of fashion items and thus can be helpful in distinguishing compatible fashion items. For example, as shown in Figure 3.1, it may be hard to predict whether the "Hybrid tank top shirt" is compatible with the "Fairy Tulle Black Skirt" with the current computer vision techniques due to their compatible color. However, if we further take the contextual descriptions into account, we can safely draw the conclusion that the lady skirt is not very suitable for the neutral top shirt. Therefore, how to model the intrinsic relatedness between the visual and contextual modalities

(a) Hybrid tank top shirt. (b) Fairy tulle black skirt.

Figure 3.1: Illustration of the importance of contextual modality in compatibility measurement.

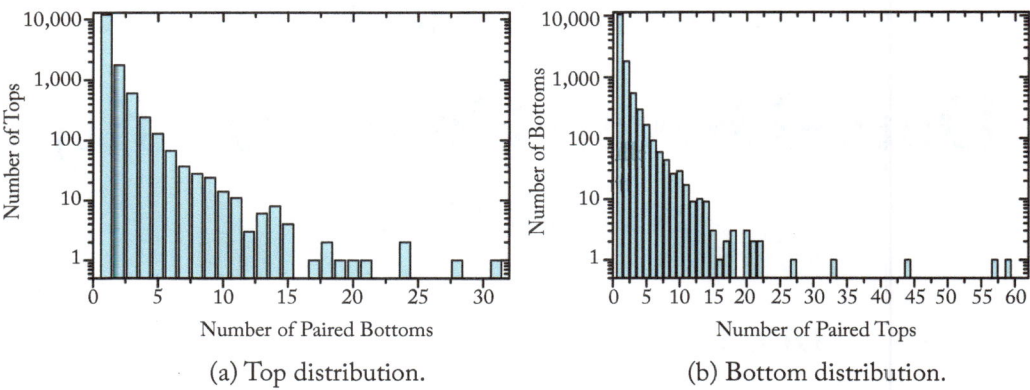

(a) Top distribution.   (b) Bottom distribution.

Figure 3.2: Distribution of tops and bottoms in our dataset. The Y-axis is in the logarithmic scale.

of the same fashion item and further boost the performance is another crucial challenge. Last but not least, according to our pilot study on Polyvore, only 1,181 (7.94%) of 14,871 fashion tops have been paired with more than 2 bottoms, as can be seen from Figure 3.2. Such a sparse relationship between fashion items makes the matrix factorization-based methods [94, 122] not applicable and hence poses another challenge for us.

To address these challenges, we present a content-based neural scheme for clothing matching (i.e., matching tops with bottoms), as shown in Figure 3.3. To deal with the sparse relationship between tops and bottoms, the proposed scheme learns a latent compatibility space to unify the complementary fashion items that come from the heterogenous spaces. In particular, the proposed scheme seamlessly integrates the multi-modal data (i.e., visual and contextual modalities) of fashion items to comprehensively model the compatibility among fashion items. Moreover, considering that the factors affecting the compatibility among items can be highly sophisticated, we employ the autoencoder neural model to exploit the latent compatibility space. Meanwhile, to take full advantage of the rich implicit semantics regarding the compatibility among fashion items on Polyvore, we further employ the advanced BPR framework [100] to exploit the pairwise preference between complementary fashion items (i.e., tops and bottoms). Ultimately, we propose a dual autoencoder network (BPR-DAE) for compatibility modeling, which jointly models the coherent relationship between different modalities of fashion items and the implicit preference among them.

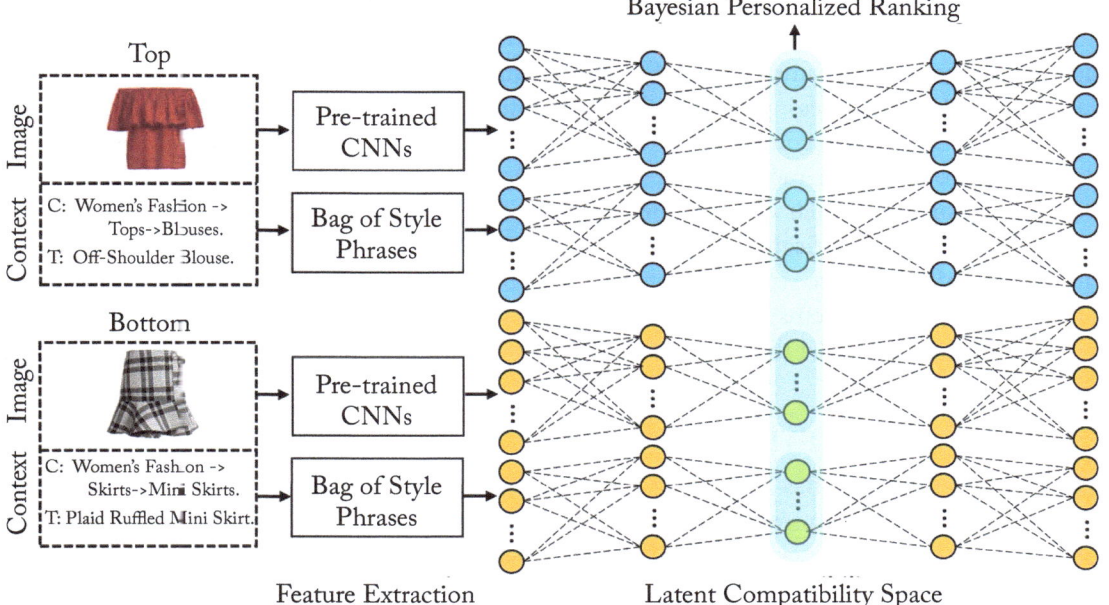

Figure 3.3: Illustration of the proposed scheme. We employ a dual autoencoder network to learn the latent compatibility space, where we jointly model the coherent relationship between visual and contextual modalities and the implicit preference among items via the Bayesian Personalized Ranking. C: category, T: title. "— >" indicates the category hierarchy.

3.2   RELATED WORK

3.2.1   FASHION ANALYSIS

The fashion domain recently has been attracting increasing attention from both the computer vision and multimedia research communities. Existing efforts mainly focus on clothing retrieval [77], clothing recommendation [42, 76], and fashionability prediction [67, 104]. For example, Liu et al. [76] proposed a latent Support Vector Machine (SVM) [21] model for an occasion-oriented outfit and item recommendation, where the dataset of wild street photos was created by human annotation. Iwata et al. [48] proposed a topic model to recommend tops for bottoms with a small dataset collected from magazines. Due to the infeasibility of a human-annotated dataset, several pioneering studies have resorted to other sources, where rich data can be harvested automatically. For example, Hu et al. [43] studied the problem of personalized whole outfit recommendation over a dataset collected from Polyvore. McAuley et al. [86] presented a general framework to model human visual preference for a pair of objects based on the Amazon co-purchase dataset. They extracted visual features with convolutional neural networks

(CNNs) and introduced a similarity metric to model the human notion of complement objects. Similarly, He et al. [34] introduced a scalable matrix factorization approach that incorporates visual signals of product images to fulfill the recommendation task. Although these researches have achieved huge success, previous efforts on fashion analysis mainly focus on the visual signals but fail to take the contextual information into consideration. To bridge this gap, Li et al. [67] proposed a multi-modal, multi-instance deep learning system to classify an given outfit as a popular or nonpopular one. Distinguished from the above research, we particularly focus on modeling the sophisticated compatibility between fashion items by seeking the nonlinear latent compatibility space with neural networks. Moreover, we seamlessly aggregate the multi-modal data of fashion items and exploit the inherent relationship between different modalities to comprehensively model the compatibility between fashion items.

3.2.2   REPRESENTATION LEARNING

Representation learning has long been an active research topic for machine learning, which aims to learn more effective representations for data, as compared to hand-designed representations, and hence achieve better performance in machine learning tasks [64]. In particular, recently, the advances in neural networks also propelled a handful of models, such as autoencoders (AE) [90], deep belief networks (DBN) [39], deep Boltzmann machine (DBM) [27], and CNNs [62] to tackle various problems. For example, Want et al. [118] utilized deep autoencoders to capture the highly nonlinear network structure and thus learn accurate network embedding. Due to the increasingly complex data and tasks, multi-view representation learning has attracted several research attempts. One basic training criterion that has been applied to multi-view representation learning is to learn a latent compact representation that can reconstruct the input as much as possible [117], where autoencoders are naturally adopted [22]. For example, Ngiam et al. [90] first proposed a structure based on multimodal autoencoders to learn the shared representation for speech and visual inputs and solve the problem of speech recognition. In addition, Wang et al. [117] proposed a multimodal deep model to learn image-text unified representations to tackle the cross-modality retrieval problem. Although representation learning has been successfully applied to solving cross modality retrieval [20, 22], phonetic recognition [117], and multilingual classification [98], limited efforts have been dedicated to the fashion domain, which is the research gap we aim to bridge in this work.

3.3   METHODOLOGY

In this section, we first introduce the notation for the following research problem formulation, and then detail the proposed BPR-DAE.

3.3.1 NOTATION

Formally, we first declare some notations. In particular, we use bold uppercase letters (e.g., $\mathbf{X}$) and bold lowercase letters (e.g., $\mathbf{x}$) to denote matrices and vectors, respectively. We employ non-bold letters (e.g., x) to represent scalars and Greek letters (e.g., β) to stand for parameters. If not clarified, all vectors are in column forms. Let $\|\mathbf{A}\|_F$ and $\|\mathbf{x}\|_2$ denote the Frobenius norm of matrix $\mathbf{A}$ and the Euclidean norm of vector $\mathbf{x}$, respectively.

3.3.2 PROBLEM FORMULATION

In a sense, people prefer to choose clothes with high compatibility, such as a silk pushy bow blouse plus a mini skirt or wool pullover plus a tweed flap skirt to make a harmonious outfit. Consequently, in this work, we focus on the compatibility modeling toward clothing matching. Suppose we have a set of tops $\mathcal{T} = \{t_1, t_2, \ldots, t_{N_t}\}$ and bottoms $\mathcal{B} = \{b_1, b_2, \ldots, b_{N_b}\}$, where N_t and N_b denote the total number of tops and bottoms, respectively. For each t_i (b_i), we use $\mathbf{v}_i^t$ ($\mathbf{v}_i^b$) $\in \mathbb{R}^{D_v}$ and $\mathbf{c}_i^t$ ($\mathbf{c}_i^b$) $\in \mathbb{R}^{D_c}$ to represent its visual and contextual input features, respectively. D_v and D_c denote the dimensions of the corresponding input features. In addition, we have a set of positive top-bottom pairs $\mathcal{S} = \{(t_{i_1}, b_{j_1}), (t_{i_2}, b_{j_2}), \ldots, (t_{i_N}, b_{j_N})\}$ extracted from the outfit compositions on Polyvore, where N denotes the number of positive pairs. Accordingly, each top t_i has a positive bottom set $\mathcal{B}_i^+ = \{b_j \in \mathcal{B} | (t_i, b_j) \in \mathcal{S}\}$. Let m_{ij} denote the compatibility between top t_i and bottom b_j. In this work, we aim to propose an accurate model to measure m_{ij}, based on which we can generate a ranking list of b_j's for a given t_i.

3.3.3 NONLINEAR COMPATIBILITY SPACE

Obviously, it is not advisable to directly measure the compatibility between fashion items from distinct spaces due to their heterogeneity. Therefore, we assume that there is a latent compatibility space that is able to bridge the gap between heterogenous fashion items, where highly compatible fashion items that share similar style, material, or functionality should also show high similarity. In fact, the factors contributing to compatibility may diversely range from style and color, to material and shape. Moreover, the relationship among these factors can be highly sophisticated. For example, a white casual T-shirt goes well with black casual jeans but not a black suit, while a pair of high boots prefers skinny leggings rather than flared pants. Toward this end, in this work, we further assume that the subtle compatibility factors lie in a highly nonlinear space, which can be learned by the advanced neural network models. In particular, we employ the autoencoder networks to learn the latent space, which has been proven to be effective in the latent space learning [118].

Autoencoder, which works in an unsupervised manner, consists of two parts: the encoder and decoder. The former maps the input data to the latent representation space, while the latter works toward mapping the latent representation space to a reconstruction space, both of which work based on multiple nonlinear functions. Suppose the encoder consists of K layers of nonlinear transformation. Given the input $\mathbf{x}$, the hidden representation for each layer can be calculated as follows:

$$\mathbf{h}_1 = s\left(\mathbf{W}_1\mathbf{x} + \mathbf{b}_1\right),$$
$$\mathbf{h}_k = s\left(\mathbf{W}_k\mathbf{h}_{k-1} + \mathbf{b}_k\right), \ k = 2, \ldots, K, \qquad (3.1)$$

where $\mathbf{h}_k$ is the hidden representation, $\mathbf{W}_k$ and $\mathbf{b}_k$, $k = 1, \ldots, K$ are the matrices of weights and biases, respectively. $s : \mathbb{R} \mapsto \mathbb{R}$ is a nonlinear function applied element wise.[1] In practice, the biases $\mathbf{b}_k$ can be horizontally merged into the weight matrix $\mathbf{W}_k$, while the input $\mathbf{x}/\mathbf{h}_k$ can be vertically appended by an entry 1. Therefore, to simplify the notation, we only consider $\mathbf{W}_k$ and ignore the bias terms in the following discussion. We treat the output of the K-th layer as the latent representation $\tilde{\mathbf{x}} = \mathbf{h}_K \in \mathbb{R}^L$, where L denotes the dimensionality of the latent representation. Then the decoder computes inversely from the latent representation $\tilde{\mathbf{x}}$ to the reconstructed representation $\hat{\mathbf{x}}$. Overall, for the input $\mathbf{x}$, the autoencoder aims to minimize the reconstruction error as follows:

$$l(\mathbf{x}) = \frac{1}{2} \left\| \hat{\mathbf{x}} - \mathbf{x} \right\|_2^2. \qquad (3.2)$$

3.3.4   COMPATIBILITY MEASURE

Apparently, visual signals play significant roles in the compatibility measure, as many visual factors such as color and shape are encoded by the visual information. Moreover, we also observed that the context of each fashion item also present important characteristics of fashion items, such as the functionality and shape. Therefore, to comprehensively measure the compatibility between fashion items, we seamlessly explore the knowledge from both visual and contextual modalities.

In particular, we first feed the visual and contextual input features of tops and bottoms to four autoencoder networks A_v^t, A_c^t, A_v^b, and A_c^b, respectively. The superscripts t and b refer to the top and bottom. We thus obtain the latent visual and contextual representation for t_i and b_j as $\tilde{\mathbf{v}}_i^t$, $\tilde{\mathbf{c}}_i^t$, $\tilde{\mathbf{v}}_j^b$, and $\tilde{\mathbf{c}}_j^b$. Then the decoder computes inversely from the latent representation to the reconstructed representation $\hat{\mathbf{v}}_i^t$, $\hat{\mathbf{c}}_i^t$, $\hat{\mathbf{v}}_j^b$, and $\hat{\mathbf{c}}_j^b$, respectively. Based on such latent visual and contextual representations of tops and bottoms, we can define the compatibility between top t_i and bottom b_j as follows:

$$m_{ij} = (1 - \beta)\left(\tilde{\mathbf{v}}_i^t\right)^T \tilde{\mathbf{v}}_j^b + \beta\left(\tilde{\mathbf{c}}_i^t\right)^T \tilde{\mathbf{c}}_j^b, \qquad (3.3)$$

where β is the non-negative trade-off parameter.

Considering the coherent relationship between items' contextual metadata and visual images, we further introduce the regularization to encourage the visual and contextual latent representation of the same fashion item x_i,

$$\mathcal{L}_{mod}\left(\tilde{\mathbf{v}}_i, \tilde{\mathbf{c}}_i\right) = -\ln\left(\sigma\left(\tilde{\mathbf{v}}_i{}^T \tilde{\mathbf{c}}_i\right)\right). \qquad (3.4)$$

---

[1] In this work, we use the sigmoid function $s(x) = \frac{1}{1+e^{-x}}$.

3.3.5   BPR-DAE

In a sense, we can easily identify the positive top-bottom pairs as which have been paired within the same outfits by fashion experts. Regarding the non-paired items (e.g., top-bottom pairs), they may just indicate the incompatibility between pairs or the missing potential positive pairs (i.e., pairs may be created in the future). Therefore, to fully take advantage of these implicit relationship between tops and bottoms, we naturally adopt the BPR framework. We assume that bottoms from the positive set $\mathcal{B}_i^+$ are more favorable to top t_i than those unobserved neutral bottoms. According to BPR, we build a training set:

$$\mathcal{D}_S := \left\{ (i, j, k) | t_i \in \mathcal{T}, b_j \in \mathcal{B}_i^+ \wedge b_k \in \mathcal{B} \backslash \mathcal{B}_i^+ \right\}, \tag{3.5}$$

where the triple (i, j, k) indicates that bottom b_j is more compatible than bottom b_k with top t_i.

Then according to [100], we have the following objective function,

$$\mathcal{L}_{bpr} = \sum_{(i,j,k) \in \mathcal{D}_S} -\ln \left(\sigma \left(m_{ijk} \right) \right), \tag{3.6}$$

where $m_{ijk} := m_{ij} - m_{ik}$, capturing the compatibility preference between top t_i, bottom b_j compared to bottom b_k, and the σ is the sigmoid function. In addition, according to Eq. (3.4) and taking the modality consistency into consideration, we have

$$\mathcal{L}_{mod} = \sum_{(i,j,k) \in \mathcal{D}_S} \left(\mathcal{L}_{mod} \left(\tilde{\mathbf{v}}_i^t, \tilde{\mathbf{c}}_i^t \right) + \mathcal{L}_{mod} \left(\tilde{\mathbf{v}}_j^b, \tilde{\mathbf{c}}_j^b \right) + \mathcal{L}_{mod} \left(\tilde{\mathbf{v}}_k^b, \tilde{\mathbf{c}}_k^b \right) \right). \tag{3.7}$$

Finally, we have the following objective function:

$$\mathcal{L} = \mathcal{L}_{bpr} + \gamma \mathcal{L}_{mod} + \mu \mathcal{L}_{rec} + \frac{\lambda}{2} \left\| \Theta \right\|_F^2, \tag{3.8}$$

where $\mathcal{L}_{rec} = \mathcal{L}_{rec}^v + \mathcal{L}_{rec}^c$, $\mathcal{L}_{rec}^v = \sum_{(i,j,k) \in \mathcal{D}_S} \left(l(\mathbf{v}_i^t) + l(\mathbf{v}_j^b) + l(\mathbf{v}_k^b) \right)$, and $\mathcal{L}_{rec}^c = \sum_{(i,j,k) \in \mathcal{D}_S} \left(l(\mathbf{c}_i^t) + l(\mathbf{c}_j^b) + l(\mathbf{c}_k^b) \right)$. μ, γ, λ are the nonnegative trade-off hyperparameters, and Θ refers to the set of parameters (i.e., $\mathbf{W}_k$ and $\hat{\mathbf{W}}_k$). The last regularizer term is designed to avoid overfitting.

3.3.6   OPTIMIZATION

Toward the optimization, the core step is to calculate the partial derivative with respect to parameters $\partial \mathcal{L} / \partial \mathbf{W}_k^{xy}$ and $\partial \mathcal{L} / \partial \hat{\mathbf{W}}_k^{xy}$, $x \in \{t, b\}$, $y \in \{v, c\}$. Due to the space limitation, we here only introduce the detailed calculation for $\partial \mathcal{L} / \partial \mathbf{W}_k^{tv}$, $\partial \mathcal{L} / \partial \hat{\mathbf{W}}_k^{tv}$, while the other partial derivative can be solved in similar fashion.

Taking advantage of the back-propagation strategy, we first calculate the $\frac{\partial \mathcal{L}_{bpr}}{\partial \mathbf{W}_K^{tv}}$, $\frac{\partial \mathcal{L}_{mod}}{\partial \mathbf{W}_K^{tv}}$, and $\frac{\partial \mathcal{L}_{rec}}{\partial \hat{\mathbf{W}}_K^{tv}}$ as follows:

$$
\begin{cases}
\dfrac{\partial \mathcal{L}_{bpr}}{\partial \mathbf{W}_K^{tv}} = -\sigma(-m_{ijk}) \dfrac{\partial(\tilde{\mathbf{v}}_i^t)}{\partial \mathbf{W}_K^{tv}} (\mathbf{v}_j^b - \mathbf{v}_k^b) \\[3mm]
\dfrac{\partial \mathcal{L}_{mod}}{\partial \mathbf{W}_K^{tv}} = -\gamma \sigma(-z_i^t) \dfrac{\partial(\tilde{\mathbf{v}}_i^t)}{\partial \mathbf{W}_K^{tv}} \tilde{\mathbf{c}}_i^t \\[3mm]
\dfrac{\partial \mathcal{L}_{rec}}{\partial \hat{\mathbf{W}}_K^{tv}} = \mu(\hat{\mathbf{v}}_i^t - \mathbf{v}_i^t) \dfrac{\partial(\hat{\mathbf{v}}_i^t)}{\partial \hat{\mathbf{W}}_K^{tv}}.
\end{cases}
\tag{3.9}
$$

As $\frac{\partial(\tilde{\mathbf{v}}_i^t)}{\partial \mathbf{W}_K^{tv}}$ and $\frac{\partial(\hat{\mathbf{v}}_i^t)}{\partial \hat{\mathbf{W}}_K^{tv}}$ can be derived from $\hat{\mathbf{v}}_i^t = \sigma(\hat{\mathbf{W}}_K^{tv} \hat{\mathbf{h}}_{K-1}^{tv} + \hat{\mathbf{b}}_K^{tv})$ and $\tilde{\mathbf{v}}_i^t = \sigma(\mathbf{W}_K^{tv} \mathbf{h}_{K-1}^{tv} + \mathbf{b}_K^{tv})$, we can easily access $\partial \mathcal{L}_{bpr}/\partial \mathbf{W}_K^{tv}$, $\partial \mathcal{L}_{mod}/\partial \mathbf{W}_K^{tv}$ and $\partial \mathcal{L}_{rec}/\partial \hat{\mathbf{W}}_K^{tv}$. Then we can iteratively obtain $\partial \mathcal{L}_{bpr}/\partial \mathbf{W}_k^{tv}$ and $\partial \mathcal{L}_{mod}/\partial \mathbf{W}_k^{tv}$, $k = K, \ldots, 1$. Meanwhile, we obtain the $\partial \mathcal{L}_{rec}/\partial \hat{\mathbf{W}}_k^{tv}$ and $\partial \mathcal{L}_{rec}/\partial \mathbf{W}_k^{tv}$, $k = K, \ldots, 1$, in the similar manner. We then employ the stochastic gradient descent to optimize the proposed model, where the network parameters can be updated as follows:

$$
\begin{cases}
\mathbf{W}_k^{tv} \leftarrow \mathbf{W}_k^{tv} - \eta \left(\dfrac{\partial \mathcal{L}_{bpr}}{\partial \mathbf{W}_k^{tv}} + \gamma \dfrac{\partial \mathcal{L}_{mod}}{\partial \mathbf{W}_k^{tv}} + \mu \dfrac{\partial \mathcal{L}_{rec}}{\partial \mathbf{W}_k^{tv}} + \lambda \mathbf{W}_k^{tv} \right) \\[3mm]
\hat{\mathbf{W}}_k^{tv} \leftarrow \hat{\mathbf{W}}_k^{tv} - \eta \left(\mu \dfrac{\partial \mathcal{L}_{rec}}{\partial \mathbf{W}_k^{kv}} + \lambda \hat{\mathbf{W}}_k^{kv} \right),
\end{cases}
\tag{3.10}
$$

where η is the learning rate.

3.4   EXPERIMENT

In this part, we conducted extensive experiments to verify our proposed BPR-DAE model on the Dataset I by answering the following research questions.

- Does BPR-DAE outperform the state-of-the-art methods?

- What is the contribution of each component of BPR-DAE?

- How does each modality contribute to the compatibility modeling?

3.4.1   EXPERIMENT SETTINGS

In this chapter, we extract the visual and contextual features of fashion items as follows.

Visual Modality. In this work, we took advantage of the advanced deep CNNs, which has been proven to be the state-of-the-art model for image representation learning [10, 55, 134]. In particular, we chose the pre-trained ImageNet deep neural network provided by the Caffe software package [51], which consists of five convolutional layers followed by three fully connected layers. We fed the image of each fashion item to the CNNs, and adopted the fc7 layer output as the visual feature. Therefore, for each item, its visual modality is represented by a 4096-D vector.

Contextual Modality. Considering the short length of such contextual information, we utilized the bag-of-words scheme [50], which has been proven to be effective to encode contextual metadata [26]. We first constructed a style vocabulary based on the categories and the words in all the titles in our dataset. As such user-generated metadata can be inevitably noisy, we thus filtered out the categories and words that appeared in less than five items as well as the words with less than three characters, which are more likely to be noise. We ultimately obtained a vocabulary of 3,529 phrases, and hence compiled the contextual modality of each fashion item with a 3,529-D boolean vector.

We separated the positive pair set S in Dataset I into three chunks: 80% of tripes for training, 10% for validation, and 10% for testing, which are denoted as S_{train}, S_{valid}, and S_{test}, respectively. Then we generated the triple set $D_{S_{train}}$, $D_{S_{valid}}$, and $D_{S_{test}}$ according to Eq. (3.5). In particular, for each positive top-bottom pair t_i and b_j, we randomly sampled M bottoms b_k's to construct M triplets (i, j, k), where $b_k \notin \mathcal{B}_i^+$ and M is set as 3. We then adopted the widely used metric AUC (Area Under the ROC curve) [99], which is defined as

$$AUC = \frac{1}{|\mathcal{T}|} \sum_i \frac{1}{E(i)} \sum_{(j,k)\in E(i)} \delta\left(m_{ij} > m_{ik}\right), \qquad (3.11)$$

where the evaluation pairs per top i are defined as

$$E(i) := \{(j,k)|(i,j) \in S_{test} \wedge (i,k) \notin S\}. \qquad (3.12)$$

$\delta(b)$ is the indicator function that returns one if the argument b is *true* and zero otherwise.

For optimization, we employed the stochastic gradient descent (SGD) [3] with the momentum factor as 0.9. We adopted the grid search strategy to determine the optimal values for the regularization parameters (i.e., λ, μ, γ) among the values $\{10^r | r \in \{-5, \ldots, -1\}\}$. In addition, the mini-batch size, the number of hidden units and learning rate for all methods were searched in $[32, 64, 128, 256, 512, 1024]$, $[128, 256, 512, 1024]$, and $[0.001, 0.01, 0.1]$, respectively. The proposed model was fine-tuned based on training set and validation set for 30 epochs, and the performance on testing set was reported. We experimentally found that the proposed model achieves the optimal performance with $K = 1$ hidden layer of 512 hidden units. All the experiments were conducted over a server equipped with four NVIDIA Titan X GPUs.

We first experimentally verified the convergence of the proposed learning algorithm. The changes of the objective function in Eq. (3.8) and the training AUC with one run of the training algorithm are illustrated in Figure 3.4. As we can see, both values first change rapidly within a few epochs and then tend to go steady finally, which well demonstrates the convergence of our model.

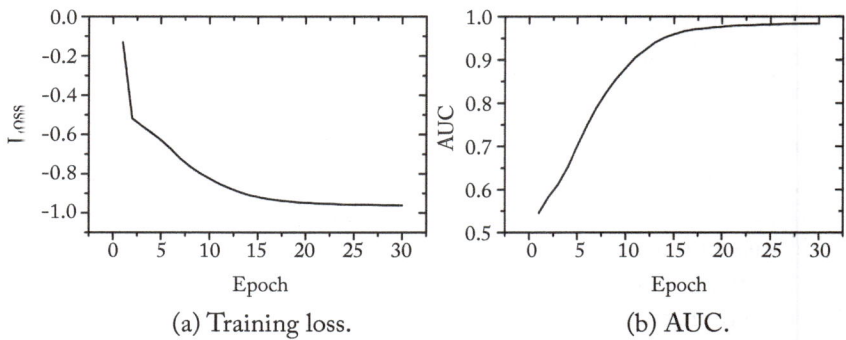

(a) Training loss.   (b) AUC.

Figure 3.4: Training loss and AUC with respect to each epoch.

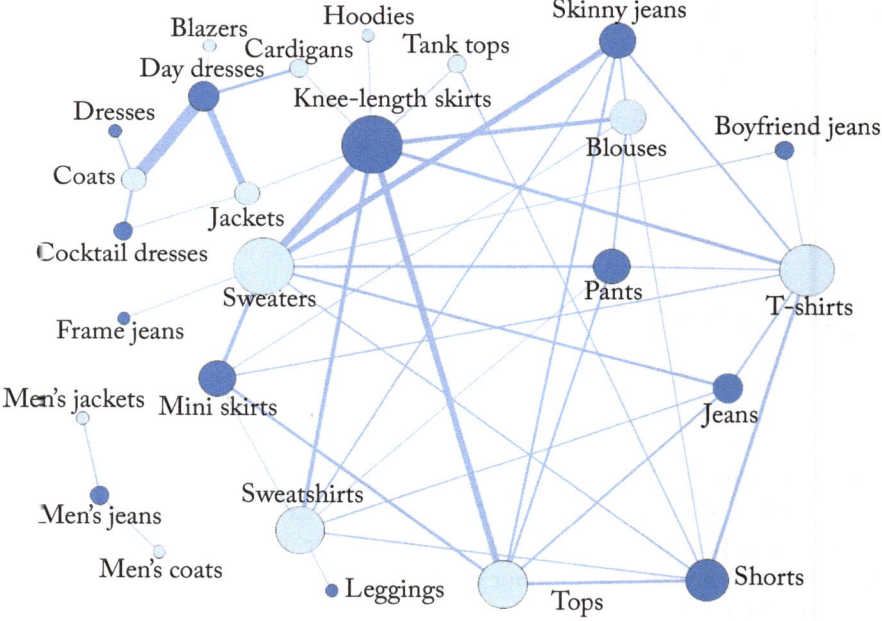

Figure 3.5: Illustration of the most popular matchings pairs between top and bottom categories.

3.4.2   DATA INSIGHTS

Due to the limited space, we only presented the most popular matching pairs of top and bottom categories[2] in our dataset in Figure 3.5. Each circle denotes a fashion category, where the light blue refers to the top categories and the dark blue denotes the bottom ones. The areas of the

---

[2]Here we only consider the category at the finest granularity for each item.

circles and the widths of the links are proportional to the number of fashion items with the given category and the co-occurrence frequency between categories, respectively. It can be seen that knee-length skirts, sweaters, and T-shirts are the most compatible items, as they are all matched with various other category items. In addition, we found that coats go more with day dresses while sweaters match more with knee-length skirts. This also implies that the contextual information regarding each fashion item can be helpful in clothing matching.

3.4.3 ON MODEL COMPARISON (RQ1)

Due to the sparsity of our dataset, where matrix factorization based methods [94, 122] are not applicable, we only considered the following content-based baselines regarding compatibility modeling to evaluate the proposed model BPR-DAE.

POP: We utilized the "popularity" of bottom b_j to measure its compatibility with top t_i. The "popularity" is defined as the number of tops that has been paired with b_j, and we thus have,

$$m_{ij} = |(i', j)|(i', j) \in \mathbf{S}_{train}|. \tag{3.13}$$

RAND: We randomly assigned the scores of m_{ij} and m_{ik} to evaluate the compatibility between items.

RAW: We measured the compatibility score between top t_i and bottom b_j based on the similarity between their raw features directly as

$$m_{ij} = \left(\mathbf{v}_i^t\right)^T \mathbf{v}_j^b + \beta \left(\mathbf{c}_i^t\right)^T \mathbf{c}_j^b. \tag{3.14}$$

IBR: We chose the image-based recommendation method proposed by [86], which aims to model the relationships between objects based on their visual appearance. This work also learns a visual style space, in which the retrieval of related objects is performed by nearest-neighbor search. Different from our model, this baseline learns the latent space by linear transformation and consider positive samples and negative samples independently. Moreover, this method only focuses on the visual information.

ExIBR: We extended IBR to handle both the visual and contextual data of fashion items, where we modified the distance function between top t_i and bottom b_j in [86] as follows:

$$d_{ij} = \left\| (\mathbf{v}_i^t - \mathbf{v}_j^b)\mathbf{Y}_v \right\|_2^2 + \beta \left\| (\mathbf{c}_i^t - \mathbf{c}_j^b)\mathbf{Y}_c \right\|_2^2, \tag{3.15}$$

where $\mathbf{Y}_v \in \mathbb{R}^{D_v \times K'}$ and $\mathbf{Y}_c \in \mathbb{R}^{D_c \times K'}$ are the projection matrices for visual and contextual modality input, respectively. K' refers to the dimension of the style space.

Table 3.1 shows the performance comparison among different approaches. From this table, we have the following observations. (1) POP achieves the worst performance, which propels us to further check the popular items in our dataset. Table 3.2 shows the five most popular tops

Table 3.1: Performance comparison of different approaches in terms of AUC

Approach	AUC
POP	0.4206
RAND	0.5094
RAW	0.5494
IBR	0.6075
ExIBR	0.7033
BPR-DAE	**0.7616**

Table 3.2: Illustration of the most popular tops and bottoms

and bottoms respectively. We noticed that the popular fashion items are all in the basic style, such as plain T-shirts and jeans, which maybe due to the fact that they can go with many other items. Therefore, we can easily find the limitations of POP method. For example, most of the popular bottoms are jeans, which maybe not suitable for professional tops and sport outfits. Therefore, it is not advisable to adopt recommendation strategy based on popularity. (2) ExIBR and BPR-DAE both outperform the visual-based baseline IBR, which confirms the necessity of considering the contextual modality in compatibility modeling. (3) BPR-DAE shows superiority over ExIBR. One possible explanation is that the highly sophisticated compatibility space would be better characterized by the autoencoder neural networks rather than by the linear transformation.

3.4.4   ON COMPONENT COMPARISON (RQ2)

To verify the effectiveness of each component of our model, we also compared BPR-DAE with the following methods.

BPR-DAE-Norec: To check the component that regularizes the reconstruction error, we removed the $\mathcal{L}_{rec}$ by setting $\mu = 0$.

BPR-DAE-Nomod: To check the modality regularizer component that controls the consistency between latent representations of different modalities, we removed the $\mathcal{L}_{mod}$ by setting $\gamma = 0$.

BPR-DAE-No: We removed both the reconstruction and modality regularizers by setting $\mu = 0$ and $\gamma = 0$.

Table 3.3 shows the performance of our model with different component configurations. It can be seen that BPR-DAE outperforms all the other derivative models, which verifies the impact of each component in our model. For example, we noticed that BPR-DAE shows superiority over BPR-DAE-Nomod, which implies that the visual and contextual information of the same fashion items does share certain consistency in terms of characterizing the fashion items. Besides, the worse performance achieved by BPR-DAE-Norec as compared to BPR-DAE suggests that the latent compatibility space can be helpful to reconstruct the fashion items.

Table 3.3: Performance comparison of our model with different component configurations with respect to AUC

Approach	AUC
BPR-DAE	**0.7616**
BPR-DAE-Norec	0.7533
BPR-DAE-Nomod	0.7539
BPR-DAE-No	0.7421

3.4.5   ON MODALITY COMPARISON (RQ3)

To verify the effectiveness of multi-modal integration, we also conducted experiments over different modality combinations. In particular, we adapted our model to BPR-DAE-V and BPR-DAE-C to cope with the visual and contextual modality of fashion items, respectively, by removing the other unnecessary autoencoder networks as well as the $\mathcal{L}_{mod}$ regularizer. Figure 3.6 shows the comparative performance of different approaches with respect to AUC. We observed that BPR-DAE outperforms both BPR-DAE-V and BPR-DAE-C, which suggests that the visual and contextual information does complement each other and both contributes to the compatibility measurement between fashion items. It is surprising that BPR-DAE-C is more effective than BPR-DAE-V. One plausible explanation is that the contextual information is more concise to present the key features of fashion items.

To intuitively illustrate the impact of contextual information, we illustrated the comparison between BPR-DAE and BPR-DAE-V on testing triplets in Figure 3.7. As can be seen, contextual metadata works better in cases where the given two bottom candidates b_j and b_k share similar visual signals, such as color or shape, where visual signals could be insufficient to

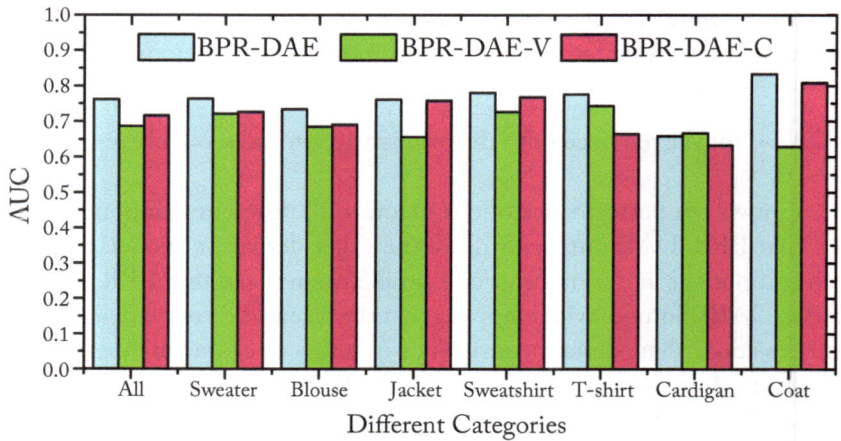

Figure 3.6: Performance of the proposed models on tops of different categories. "All" refers to the whole testing set.

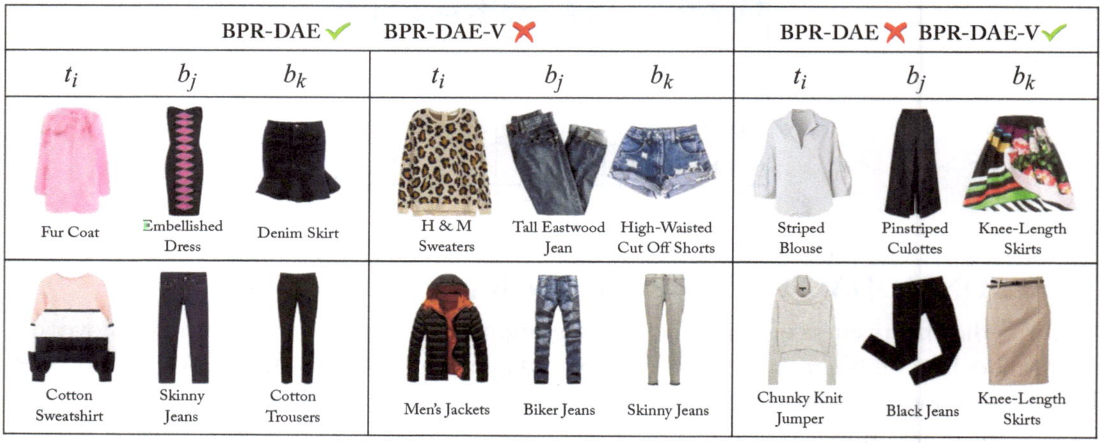

BPR-DAE ✔		BPR-DAE-V ✘			BPR-DAE ✘ BPR-DAE-V ✔		
t_i	b_j	b_k	t_i	b_j	b_k	t_i	b_j	b_k

| Fur Coat | Embellished Dress | Denim Skirt | H & M Sweaters | Tall Eastwood Jean | High-Waisted Cut Off Shorts | Striped Blouse | Pinstriped Culottes | Knee-Length Skirts |
| Cotton Sweatshirt | Skinny Jeans | Cotton Trousers | Men's Jackets | Biker Jeans | Skinny Jeans | Chunky Knit Jumper | Black Jeans | Knee-Length Skirts |

Figure 3.7: Illustration of the comparison between BPR-DAE and BPR-DAE-V on testing triples. All the triples satisfy $m_{ij} > m_{ik}$. Due to the limited space, we only list the key phrases of items' contextual metadata.

distinguish the compatibility between them with the given top t_i. Nevertheless, such contextual information may also lead to certain failed triplets due to the category matching bias, especially when visual signals of bottom candidates differ significantly. For example, it is popular to match blouses with knee-length skirts according to our dataset, which may thus lead to the first failed testing triplet in the right most column.

To obtain more detailed insights, apart from the overall comparative evaluation, we further checked the performance of the proposed models on the seven most popular top categories. As can be seen from Figure 3.6, BPR-DAE still consistently shows superiority over both BPR-DAE-V and BPR-DAE-C on each of the seven top categories. Meanwhile, we found that contextual information significantly improves the performance on top categories such as "Jacket" and "Coat," compared to "T-shirt" and "Cardigan" categories. One possible explanation is that the matching for coats and jackets would be more complicated [19] due to the fact that they serve people in more seasons and thus apart from the common color and pattern factors, we also need further consider other factors such as various material (e.g., silk, wool, fur, and leather) and length (e.g., long, medium, and short). These factors may not be easy-learned from visual signals but can be effectively captured by contextual information. On the contrary, pertaining to tops of basic style categories, such as T-shirts and cardigans, where color and shape factors play more important roles in clothing matching, visual signals are more powerful than the context.

3.4.6   ON COMPLEMENTARY FASHION ITEM RETRIEVAL

To efficiently evaluate the proposed BPR-DAE toward the complementary fashion item retrieval, we adopted the common strategy [37, 59] that feeds each top t_i appeared in $\mathcal{S}_{test}$ as a query, and randomly selects T bottoms as the candidates, where there is only one positive candidate. Then by passing them to the neural networks trained by $\mathcal{S}_{train}$ and $\mathcal{S}_{valid}$, getting their latent representations and calculating the compatibility score m_{ij} according to Eq. (3.3), we can generate a ranking list of these bottoms for the given top. In our setting, we care about the average position of the positive bottom in the ranking list and thus adopt the mean reciprocal rank (MRR) metric [52], which provides insights into the ability to return the positive bottoms at the top of the rankings. In total, we have 1,954 unique tops in the testing set, among which 1,262 tops have never appeared in $\mathcal{S}_{train}$ or $\mathcal{S}_{valid}$.

Figure 3.3 shows the performance of different models in terms of MRR at different numbers of the bottom candidates T. It is worth mentioning that we dropped the POP baseline here due to the fact that the majority of tops share the same popularity of 1, which makes it intractable to generate the ranking. As can be seen, our model shows superiority over all the other baselines consistently at different numbers of bottom candidates, which verifies the effectiveness of our model in complementary fashion item retrieval and coping with the cold start problem. Certain intuitive ranking results for testing tops can be found in Figure 3.9. We noticed that although BPR-DAE sometimes failed to accurately rank the positive bottom at the first place, the neutral bottoms ranked before the positive one are also compatible with the given top, which is reasonable in the real application.

3.5   SUMMARY

In this chapter, we present a content-based neural scheme (BPR-DAE) for compatibility modeling toward clothing matching (i.e., matching the tops and bottoms), which is able to jointly

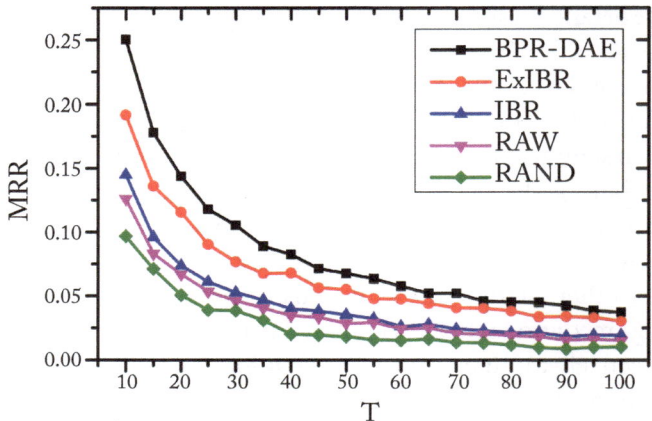

Figure 3.8: Performance of different models with respect to MRR at different numbers of the bottom candidates T.

Figure 3.9: Illustration of the ranking results for given testing tops. The bottoms highlighted in the red boxes are the positive ones.

model the coherent relationship between different modalities of fashion items and the implicit preference among items via a dual autoencoder network. Experimental results demonstrate the effectiveness of our proposed scheme and verify the advantages of taking the contextual modality into consideration in terms of compatibility modeling. Surprisingly, we found that contextual modality even shows superiority over the visual modality, especially toward complicated tops (e.g., coats) rather than the basic ones (e.g., T-shirts). Currently, we fail to explore the category hierarchy to further enhance the compatibility modeling, which can be the future work direction.

CHAPTER 4

Knowledge-Guided Compatibility Modeling

4.1 INTRODUCTION

Beyond the pure data-driven compatibility modeling as introduced in Chapter 3, this chapter presents the knowledge-guided compatibility modeling. As a matter of fact, most existing researches mainly rely on the deep neural networks to extract the effective representations for fashion items to tackle the clothing matching problem, due to their impressive advances in various research domains, including the image classification, speech recognition, and machine translation. However, as pure data-driven methods, neural networks not only suffer from the poor interpretability but also overlook the value of human knowledge. Especially, as an essential aspect of people's daily life, the clothing matching domain has accumulated various valuable knowledge, i.e., the matching rules. Although they may be of high subjectivity, certain matching rules have been widely accepted by the public as common sense. For example, tank tops would go better with shorts instead of the dress, while silk tops better avoid the knit bottoms. Therefore, it is highly desirable to devise an effective model to seamlessly incorporate such domain knowledge into the pure data-driven learning methods and hence boost the matching performance.

In this work, we aim to investigate the practical fashion problem of clothing matching by leveraging both the deep neural networks and the rich human knowledge in fashion domain. In fact, the problem we pose here can be cast as the compatibility modeling between the complementary fashion items, such as tops and bottoms. However, comprehensively model the compatibility between fashion items from both the data-driven and knowledge-driven perspectives is non-trivial due to the following challenges: (1) the human knowledge pertaining to fashion is usually implicitly conveyed by the compositions of fashion experts, which makes the domain knowledge unstructured and fuzzy. Therefore, how to construct a set of structured knowledge rules for the clothing matching constitutes a tough challenge; (2) how to seamlessly encode such knowledge rules into the pure data-driven learning framework and enable the model to learn from not only the specific data but also the general rules poses another challenge for us; and (3) for different samples, knowledge rules may present different levels of confidence and hence provide different levels of guidance. For example, as can be seen from Figure 4.1, both compositions satisfy the rule "stripe tops can go with stripe bottoms" according to their contextual metadata. However, obviously, the given rule should impose more regularization toward the example of

Stripe Roll   Striped Midi   White Striped   Skirt in Black
Neck   Skirt   Crop Top   Stripes

(a) Example 1.   (b) Example 2.

Figure 4.1: Illustration of the rule confidence on different item pairs. Both examples satisfy the rule "stripe tops can go with stripe bottoms."

Figure 4.1a and deserve higher rule confidence as compared to that of Figure 4.1b. Accordingly, how to effectively assign the rule confidence is a crucial challenge.

To address the aforementioned challenges, we present a compatibility modeling scheme with attentive knowledge distillation, dubbed as AKD-DBPR, as shown in Figure 4.2, which is able to learn from both the specific data samples and the general domain knowledge. In particular, we adopt the teacher-student scheme [45] to incorporate the domain knowledge (as a teacher) and enhance the performance of neural networks (as a student). As a pure data-driven learning, the student network aims to learn a latent compatibility space to unify the fashion items from heterogenous spaces with dual-path neural networks. To comprehensively model the compatibility and the semantic relation between different modalities, the student network seamlessly integrates the visual and contextual modalities of fashion items by imposing hidden layers over the concatenated vectors of visual and contextual representations. Moreover, to better characterize the relative compatibility between fashion items, we investigate the pairwise preference between complementary fashion items by building our student network based on the BPR framework [100]. Meanwhile, we encode the domain knowledge with a set of flexible structured logic rules and encode these knowledge rules into the teacher network with regularizers, whereby we introduce the attention mechanism to attentively assign the rule confidence. Ultimately, the student network is encouraged to not only achieve good performance of the compatibility modeling but also emulate the rule-regularized teacher network well.

4.2   RELATED WORK

4.2.1   COMPATIBILITY MODELING

As mentioned in Chapter 3, increasing research attentions have been paid to the fashion domain, especially the compatibility modeling between fashion items [31, 67, 86, 108] in fashion analysis. Overall, existing studies mainly focus on modeling the compatibility purely based on the data-driven deep learning methods but overlook the value of domain knowledge. Distinguished from

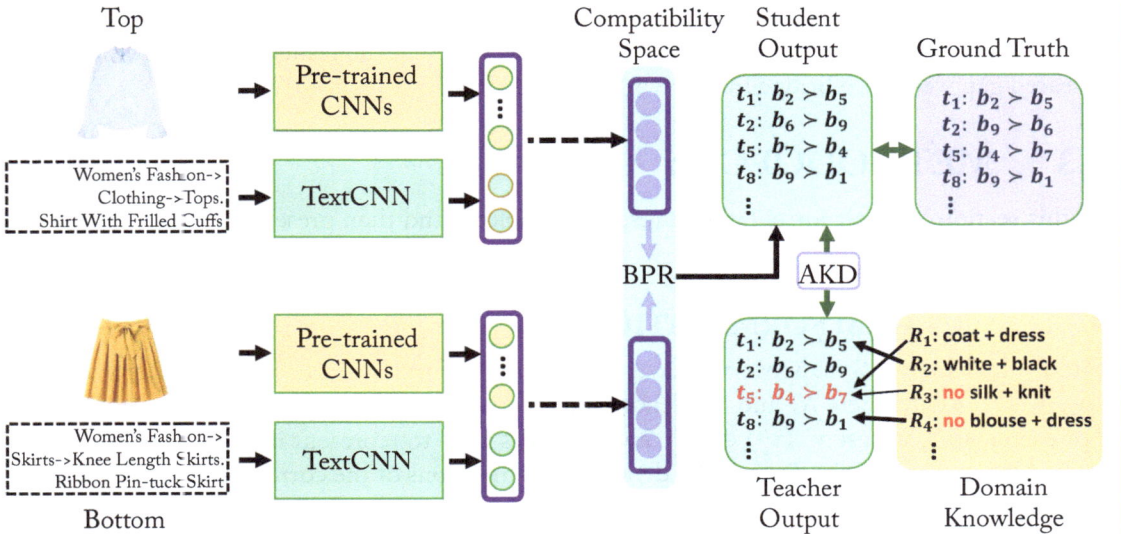

Figure 4.2: Illustration of the proposed scheme. The student network, consisting of dual-path neural networks, aims to learn the latent compatibility space where the implicit preference among items can be modeled via BPR. The teacher network encodes the domain knowledge and guides the student network via attentive knowledge distillation (AKD). t_i: top, b_j: bottom, "$\succ$": pair-wise preference. "$->$" denotes the category hierarchy. The width of the arrows originated from rules refers to the rule confidence.

these researches, we aim to explore the potential of the fashion domain knowledge to guide the pure data-driven neural networks and improve the interpretability as a side product.

4.2.2   KNOWLEDGE DISTILLATION

Although deep neural networks have harvested huge success in a variety of application domains ranging from natural language processing to computer vision [11, 108, 130], several researchers still have certain concerns with the poor interpretability as pure data-driven models. Toward this end, one mainstream research is to take advantage of the additional knowledge as a guidance to train the traditional neural networks. Hinton et al. [40] first introduced a knowledge distillation framework to transfer the knowledge from a large cumbersome model to a small model. Inspired by this, Hu et al. [45] introduced an iterative teacher-student distillation approach, which combines neural networks with several first-order logic rules representing structured knowledge in the domain of natural language processing. Later, Yu et al. [131] proposed to utilize the knowledge of linguistic statistics to regularize the learning process in the context of visual relationship detection. Although knowledge distillation in deep neural networks has been successfully applied to solving the visual relationship detection [131], sentence sentiment analysis, and name entity recognition [98], limited efforts have been dedicated to the fashion domain, which is the research gap we aim to bridge in this work.

4.3   METHODOLOGY

In this section, we first formulate the research problem, and then present the proposed AKD-DBPR.

4.3.1   PROBLEM FORMULATION

Similar to Chapter 3, suppose we have a set of tops $\mathcal{T} = \{t_1, t_2, \ldots, t_{N_t}\}$ and bottoms $\mathcal{B} = \{b_1, b_2, \ldots, b_{N_b}\}$, where N_t and N_b denote the total numbers of tops and bottoms, respectively. For each t_i (b_i), we use $\mathbf{v}_i^t$ ($\mathbf{v}_i^b$) $\in \mathbb{R}^{D_v}$ and $\mathbf{c}_i^t$ ($\mathbf{c}_i^b$) $\in \mathbb{R}^{D_c}$ to represent its visual and contextual embeddings, respectively. D_v and D_c denote the dimensions of the corresponding embeddings. In addition, we have a set of positive top-bottom pairs $\mathcal{S} = \{(t_{i_1}, b_{j_1}), (t_{i_2}, b_{j_2}), \ldots, (t_{i_N}, b_{j_N})\}$ derived from our Dataset I, where N is the total number of positive pairs. Accordingly, for each top t_i, we can derive a set of positive bottoms $\mathcal{B}_i^+ = \{b_j \in \mathcal{B} | (t_i, b_j) \in \mathcal{S}\}$. Meanwhile, we have a set of rules $\mathcal{R} = \{R_l\}_{l=1}^L$ pertaining to clothing matching, where R_l is the l-th rule and L is the total number of rules. We employ $\mathcal{R}^+$ and $\mathcal{R}^-$ denote the set of positive and negative rules, respectively. We employ m_{ij} to denote the compatibility between top t_i and bottom b_j. To accurately measure m_{ij}, we focus on devising a neural compatibility modeling scheme, which is able to jointly learn from both the specific data samples and general knowledge rules.

4.3.2   DATA-DRIVEN COMPATIBILITY MODELING

Similar to the previous chapter, we assume that there is a latent compatibility space that can bridge the gap between fashion items from heterogeneous spaces. In such latent space, compatible complementary fashion items are enabled to share high similarity. In particular, we adopt the pure data-driven neural network to explore the latent compatibility space, due to its recent compelling success in various machine learning applications.

As previously mentioned that each fashion item can be associated with multiple modalities (i.e., the visual and contextual modalities), to seamlessly exploit the potential of both modalities in the compatibility modeling, we employ the multi-layer perceptron (MLP) to model the semantic relation between different modalities of the same fashion items. In particular, we add K hidden layers over the concatenated vectors of visual and contextual representations as follows:

$$\begin{cases} \mathbf{z}_{i0}^x = \begin{bmatrix} \mathbf{v}_i^x \\ \mathbf{c}_i^x \end{bmatrix}, \\ \mathbf{z}_{i1}^x = s(\mathbf{W}_1^x \mathbf{z}_{i0}^x + \mathbf{b}_1^x), \\ \mathbf{z}_{ik}^x = s(\mathbf{W}_k^x \mathbf{z}_{i(k-1)}^x + \mathbf{b}_k^x), \ k = 2, \ldots, K, x = \{t, b\}, \end{cases} \tag{4.1}$$

where $\mathbf{z}_{ik}^x$ denotes the hidden representation, $\mathbf{W}_k^x$ and $\mathbf{b}_k^x$, $k = 1, \ldots, K$, are weight matrices and biases, respectively. The superscripts t and b refer to *top* and *bottom*. $s : \mathbb{R} \mapsto \mathbb{R}$ is a nonlinear function applied element wise.[1] We treat the output of the K-th layer as the latent representations for tops and bottoms, i.e., $\tilde{\mathbf{z}}_i^x = \mathbf{z}_{iK}^x \in \mathbb{R}^{D_l}$, $x = \{t, b\}$, where D_l denotes the dimensionality of the latent compatibility space. Accordingly, we can measure the compatibility between top t_i and bottom b_j as follows:

$$m_{ij} = \left(\tilde{\mathbf{z}}_i^t\right)^T \tilde{\mathbf{z}}_j^b. \tag{4.2}$$

In this chapter, we also adopt the BPR framework that has proven to be powerful in the implicit preference modeling [6, 36]. In particular, we assume that bottoms from the positive set $\mathcal{B}_i^+$ are more compatible to top t_i than those non-composed neutral bottoms. Accordingly, we build the following training set:

$$\mathcal{D}_S := \left\{ (i, j, k) | t_i \in \mathcal{T}, b_j \in \mathcal{B}_i^+ \wedge b_k \in \mathcal{B} \backslash \mathcal{B}_i^+ \right\}, \tag{4.3}$$

where the triplet (i, j, k) refers to that bottom b_j is more compatible with top t_i compared to bottom b_k.

Then according to [100], we have the objective function,

$$\begin{aligned} \mathcal{L}_{bpr} &= \sum_{(i,j,k)\in\mathcal{D}_S} \mathcal{L}_{bpr}\left(m_{ij}, m_{ik}\right) \\ &= \sum_{(i,j,k)\in\mathcal{D}_S} -\ln\left(\sigma\left(m_{ij} - m_{ik}\right)\right) + \frac{\lambda}{2}\left\|\Theta\right\|_F^2, \end{aligned} \tag{4.4}$$

where λ is the non-negative hyperparameter, the last term is designed to avoid overfitting and Θ refers to the set of parameters (i.e., $\mathbf{W}_k^x$ and $\mathbf{b}_k^x$) of neural networks.

4.3.3 ATTENTIVE KNOWLEDGE DISTILLATION

As an important aspect of people's daily life, clothing matching has gradually accumulated much valuable human knowledge. For example, it is favorable that a coat goes better with a dress than with short pants, while a silk top can hardly go with a knit bottom. In order to fully leverage the valuable domain knowledge, we utilize the knowledge distillation technique to guide the neural networks and allow the model to learn from general rules [45]. In particular, we adopt the teacher-student scheme, whose underlying intuition is analogous to the human education, where the teacher is aware of several professional rules and he/she thus can instruct students with his/her solutions to particular questions. In this work, considering the flexibility of logic rules [23] as a declarative language, we use logic rules to represent the fashion domain knowledge. We encode these rules via regularization terms into a teacher network q, which can be

---

[1] In this work, we use the sigmoid function $s(x) = 1/(1 + e^{-x})$.

further employed to guide the training of the student network p of interest (i.e., the aforementioned data-driven neural network designed for compatibility modeling). Ultimately, we aim to achieve a good balance between the superior prediction performance of student network p and the mimic capability of student network p to teacher network q. Accordingly, we have the objective formulation at iteration t as

$$\boldsymbol{\Theta}^{(t+1)} = \arg\min_{\boldsymbol{\Theta}} \sum_{(i,j,k) \in \mathcal{D}_S} \left\{ (1-\rho)\mathcal{L}_{bpr}\left(m_{ij}^p, m_{ik}^p\right) \right.$$
$$\left. + \rho\mathcal{L}_{crs}\left(\mathbf{q}^{(t)}(i,j,k), \mathbf{p}(i,j,k)\right) \right\} + \frac{\lambda}{2}\|\boldsymbol{\Theta}\|_F^2 , \qquad (4.5)$$

where $\mathcal{L}_{crs}$ stands for the cross-entropy loss, $\mathbf{p}(i,j,k)$ and $\mathbf{q}(i,j,k)$ refer to the sum-normalized distribution over the compatibility scores predicted by the student network p and teacher network q, (i.e., $[m_{ij}^p, m_{ik}^p]$ and $[m_{ij}^q, m_{ik}^q]$), respectively. ρ is the imitation parameter calibrating the relative importance of these two objectives.

4.3.4   TEACHER NETWORK CONSTRUCTION

As the teacher network plays a pivotal role in the knowledge distillation process, we now proceed to introduce the derivation of the teacher network q. On the one hand, we expect that the student network p can learn well from the teacher network q and this property can be naturally measured by the closeness between the compatibility prediction of both networks p and q. On the other hand, we attempt to utilize the rule regularizer to encode the general domain knowledge. In particular, we adapt the teacher network construction method proposed in [45, 46] as follows:

$$\min_{\mathbf{q}} KL(\mathbf{q}(i,j,k) \parallel \mathbf{p}(i,j,k)) - C\sum_{l} \mathbb{E}_{\mathbf{q}}[\mathbf{f}_l(i,j,k)], \qquad (4.6)$$

where C is the balance regularization parameter and KL measures the KL-divergence between $\mathbf{p}(i,j,k)$ and $\mathbf{q}(i,j,k)$. This formulation has proven to be a convex problem and can be optimized with the following closed-form solutions,

$$\mathbf{q}^*(i,j,k) \propto \mathbf{p}(i,j,k) \exp\left\{ \sum_{l} C\lambda_l \mathbf{f}_l(i,j,k) \right\}, \qquad (4.7)$$

where λ_l stands for the confidence of the l-th rule and the larger λ_l indicates the stronger rule constraint. $\mathbf{f}_l(i,j,k)$ is the l-th rule constraint function devised to reward the predictions of the student network that meet the rules while penalize the others. In our work, given the sample (i,j,k), we expect to reward the compatibility m_{ij}, if (i,j) satisfies the positive rule but (i,k) not or (i,k) triggers the negative rule while (i,j) not. In particular, we define $f_l^{ij}(i,j,k)$, the element of $\mathbf{f}_l(i, j, k)$ calibrating m_{ij}, as follows:

$$f_l^{ij}(i, j, k) = \begin{cases} 1, & \text{if} \begin{cases} \delta_l(ij) = 1, \delta_l(ik) = 0, l \in \mathcal{R}^+, \\ \delta_l(ij) = 0, \delta_l(ik) = 1, l \in \mathcal{R}^-, \end{cases} \\ 0, & \text{others,} \end{cases} \tag{4.8}$$

where $\delta_l(ab) = 1(0)$ means that the sample (a, b) satisfies the l-th rule (or not). We define the other element $f_l^{ik}(i, j, k)$ of $\mathbf{f}_l(i, j, k)$ corresponding m_{ik} in the same manner.

Traditionally, λ_l in Eq. (4.7) can be either manually assigned or automatically learned from the data, and both ways assume the rules have universal confidence to all samples. However, in fact, different rules may have different confidence levels for different samples, which can be attributed to the fact that the human knowledge rules can be general and fuzzy. It is intractable to directly pre-define the universal rule confidence. Therefore, considering that different rules can flexibly contribute to the guidance to the given samples, we adopt the attention mechanism [1], which has proven to be effective in many machine learning tasks such as the recommendation [7, 11] and representation learning [95]. The key to the success of attention mechanism lies in the observation that human tends to selectively attend to parts of the input signal rather than the entirety at once during the process of human recognition. In our work, we adopt the soft attention model to assign the rule confidence adaptively according to the given samples. In particular, for a given sample (i, j, k) and the set of rules it activates $\mathcal{R}(i, j, k)$, we assign $\lambda_l(i, j, k)$ as follows:

$$\lambda_l'(i, j, k) = \mathbf{w}^T \phi \left(\mathbf{W}_t \left[\tilde{\mathbf{v}}_i, \tilde{\mathbf{c}}_i \right] + \mathbf{W}_b \left[\tilde{\mathbf{v}}_j, \tilde{\mathbf{c}}_j \right] + \mathbf{W}_b \left[\tilde{\mathbf{v}}_k, \tilde{\mathbf{c}}_k \right] \right.$$
$$\left. + \mathbf{W}_l \mathbf{r}_l + \mathbf{b} \right) + c, \quad l \in \mathcal{R}(i, j, k), \tag{4.9}$$

where the $\mathbf{W}_t \in \mathbb{R}^{h \times (D_v + D_t)}$, $\mathbf{W}_b \in \mathbb{R}^{h \times (D_v + D_t)}$, $\mathbf{W}_l \in \mathbb{R}^{h \times L}$, $\mathbf{w} \in \mathbb{R}^h$, $\mathbf{b} \in \mathbb{R}^h$, and c are the model parameters. h represents the hidden layer size of the attention network. $\mathbf{r}_l \in \mathbb{R}^L$ stands for the one-hot encoding of the l-th rule. The attention scores are then normalized as follows:

$$\lambda_l(i, j, k) = \frac{\exp\left(\lambda_l'(i, j, k)\right)}{\sum_{u \in \mathcal{R}(i, j, k)} \exp\left(\lambda_u'(i, j, k)\right)}. \tag{4.10}$$

Figure 4.3 illustrates the workflow of our model, while the optimization procedure of our framework is summarized in Algorithm 4.1. Notably, the teacher network is first constructed from the student network at the very beginning of the training, which may induce the poor guidance at first. Therefore, we expect the whole framework favors to the prediction of the ground truth more at the initial stage but gradually bias toward the imitate capability of the student network to the teacher network. Therefore, we adopt the parameter assigning strategy in [45] to assign ρ dynamically, which keeps ρ increasing as the training process goes.

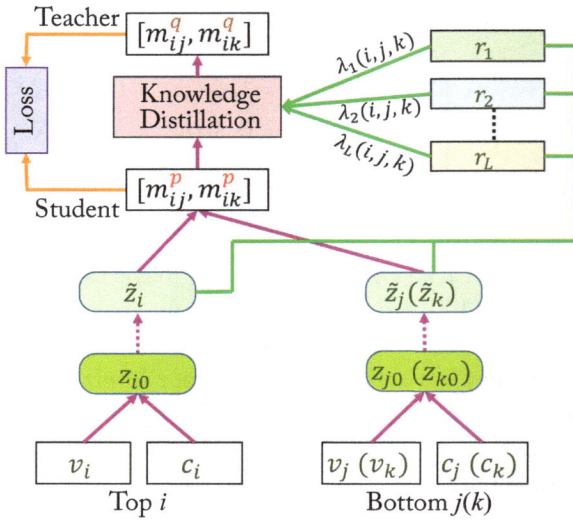

Figure 4.3: Workflow of the proposed attentive knowledge distillation framework.

Algorithm 4.1 Attentive Knowledge Distillation.

Input: $\mathcal{D}_S = \{(i, j, k)\}, \mathcal{R} = \{(R_l)\}_{l=1}^{L}, \rho, C$
Output: Parameters Θ in the student network p, parameters Φ in the attention network a.
1: Initialize neural network parameters Θ and Φ.
2: **repeat**
3:   Draw (i, j, k) from $\mathcal{D}_S$
4:   **for** each l in $\mathcal{R}(i, j, k)$ **do**
5:     Compute $\lambda_l(i, j, k)$ according to Eqs. (4.9) and (4.10).
6:   **end for**
7:   Construct teacher network q according to Eq. (4.7).
8:   Transfer knowledge into p by updating Θ and Φ according to Eq. (4.5).
9: **until** Converge

4.3.5 RULE CONSTRUCTION

In this work, we aim to leverage the explicit structured domain knowledge to guide the student neural network and hence boost the performance. To derive the domain knowledge, we first exploit our internal training dataset, which contains rich positive top-bottom pairs. In general, the compatibility between fashion items is mainly affected by five attributes: color, material, pattern, category, and brand. We hence define a dictionary with the possible values of each attribute based on the training dataset while taking the annotation details in [84] as a reference. Due to the limited space, Table 4.1 shows several value examples of each attribute.[2] We then calculate the co-occurrence of the value pairs for each attribute and retain both the top 10 and the last 10 pairs as the rule candidates, as we assume that the high co-occurrence can indicate the high compatibility and facilitate the screen of positive rules, e.g., "black top goes better with a black bottom," while the low co-occurrence may contribute to the derivation of the negative rules, such as "blouse cannot go with the dress." The underlying philosophy behind is that sometimes it is intractable to identify compatible fashion items but effortless to determine the incompatible ones. Thereafter, to ensure the quality of these rules extracted from the limited dataset, we further ask three fashion-lovers to manually screen the rules. Finally, we obtain 15 rules, which we will be detailed in the following section.

Table 4.1: Value examples of each attribute

Attributes	Value Examples
Color	Black, white, green, red, blue, grey
Material	Knit, silk, leather, cotton, fur, cashmere
Pattern	Pure, grid, dot, floral, number (letter)
Category	Coat, dress, skirt, sweater, jeans, hoodie
Brand	Yoins, HM, Topshop, Gucci

For simplicity, we use "$value1 + value2$" to denote the positive rule, while "no $value1 + value2$" representing the negative rule. For example, "black + black" stands for the positive rule "black tops can go with black bottoms," and "no silk + knit" represents the negative rule "silk tops cannot go with knit bottoms." According to Eq. (4.8), our model needs to determine whether the pair of t_i and b_j activates the given rule. We hence argue that (t_i, b_j) satisfies the (positive/negative) rule, if the $value1$ and $value2$ of the rule, respectively, appear in the contextual metadata of t_i and b_j.

4.4   EXPERIMENT

To evaluate the proposed method, we conducted extensive experiments on the real-world Dataset I by answering the following research questions.

- Does AKD-DBPR outperform the state-of-the-art methods?

- How do the attention mechanisms affect the performance?

- How does AKD-DBPR perform in the application of the complementary fashion item retrieval?

[2]The complete list can be accessed via https://ilearnfashion.wixsite.com/compatibility-model/.

In this section, we first introduce the experiment setting and then provide the experiment results as well as discussion on each above research question.

4.4.1   EXPERIMENT SETTINGS

In this chapter, we extract the visual and contextual representations of fashion items as follows.

Visual Modality. Regarding the visual modality, similar to our previous work, we adopted the pre-trained ImageNet deep neural network provided by the Caffe software package [51], which consists of five convolutional layers followed by three fully connected layers. We represented the visual modality of each item with the 4096-D output vector of the fc7 layer.

Contextual Modality. In this work, contextual description of each fashion item refers to its title and category labels in different granularity. To obtain the effective contextual representation, instead of the traditional linguistic features [106, 107], we adopted the CNN architecture [57], which has achieved compelling performance in various natural language processing tasks [102]. In particular, we first represented each contextual description as a concatenated word vector, where each row represents one constituent word and each word is represented by the publicly available 300-D word2vec vector. We then deployed the single-channel CNN, consisting of a convolutional layer on top of the concatenated word vectors and a max pooling layer. In particular, we had four kernels with sizes of 2, 3, 4, and 5, 100 feature maps for each and the rectified linear unit (ReLU) as the activation function. Ultimately, we obtained a 400-D contextual representation for each item.

We divided the positive pair set S into three chunks: 80% of triplets for training, 10% for validation, and 10% for testing, denoted as S_{train}, S_{valid}, and S_{test}, respectively. We then generated the triplets $\mathcal{D}_{S_{train}}$, $\mathcal{D}_{S_{valid}}$, and $\mathcal{D}_{S_{test}}$ according to Eq. (4.3). For each positive pair of t_i and b_j, we randomly sampled M bottoms b_k's and each b_k contributes to a triplet (i, j, k), where $b_k \notin \mathcal{B}_i^+$ and M is set as 3. We adopted the area under the ROC curve (AUC) [133] as the evaluation metric. For optimization, we employed the stochastic gradient descent (SGD) [3] with the momentum factor as 0.9. We adopted the grid search strategy to determine the optimal values for the regularization parameters (i.e., λ, C) among the values $\{10^r | r \in \{-4, \dots, -1\}\}$ and $[2, 4, 6, 8]$, respectively. In addition, the mini-batch size, the number of hidden units, and learning rate were searched in $[32, 64, 128, 256]$, $[128, 256, 512, 1024]$, and $[0.01, 0.05, 0.1]$, respectively. The proposed model was fine-tuned for 40 epochs, and the performance on the testing set was reported. We empirically found that the proposed model achieves the optimal performance with $K = 1$ hidden layer of 1,024 hidden units.

We first experimentally verified the convergence of the proposed learning scheme. Figure 4.4 shows the changes of the objective function in Eq. (4.5) and the training AUC with one iteration of our algorithm. As we can see, both values first change rapidly in a few epochs and then go steady finally, which well demonstrates the convergence of our model.

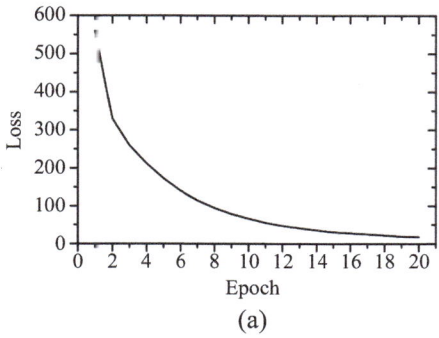 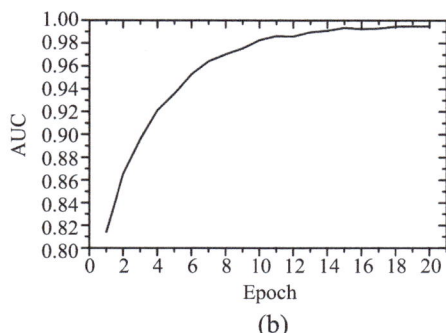

(a)   (b)

Figure 4.4: Training loss and the AUC curves.

4.4.2   ON MODEL COMPARISON (RQ1)

Due to the sparsity of our dataset, where matrix factorization-based methods [14, 15, 94, 122] are not applicable, we chose the following content-based baselines regarding compatibility modeling to evaluate the proposed model AKD-DBPR.

- **POP**: We used the "popularity" of bottom b_j to measure its compatibility with top t_i. Here the "popularity" is defined as the number of tops that has been paired with b_j in the training set.

- **RAND**: We randomly assigned the compatibility scores of m_{ij} and m_{ik} between items.

- **IBR**: We chose the image-based recommendation method proposed by [86], which aims to model the compatibility between objects based on their visual appearance. This method learns a latent style space, where the retrieval of related objects can be performed by traditional nearest-neighbor search. Different from our model, this baseline learns the latent space by simple linear transformation and only consider the visual information of fashion items.

- **ExIBR**: We adopted the extension of IBR in [108], which is able to handle both the visual and contextual data of fashion items.

- **BPR-DAE**: We selected the content-based neural scheme introduced by [108], which is capable of jointly modeling the coherent relation between different modalities of fashion items and the implicit preference among items via a dual autoencoder network.

- **DBPR**: To get a better understanding of our model, we introduced the baseline DBPR, which is the derivation of our model by removing the guidance of the teacher network and solely relies on the student network.

Since we can choose either the distilled student network p or the teacher network q with a final projection according to Eq. (4.7) for the testing, we introduced two derivations of our model: AKD-DBPR-p and AKD-DBPR-q. Here p (q) means to use the final student (teacher) network to calculate the compatibility between items.

Table 4.2 shows the performance comparison among different approaches. From this table, we have the following observations. (1) DBPR outperforms all the other state-of-the-art pure data-driven baselines, which indicates the superiority of the proposed content-based neural networks for compatibility modeling. (2) AKD-DBPR-p and AKD-DBPR-q both surpass DBPR, which validates the benefit of knowledge distillation in the context of compatibility modeling. To intuitively understand the impact of the rule guidance, we illustrate the comparison between AKD-DBPR and DBPR on several testing triplets in Figure 4.5. As we can see, AKD-DBPR performs especially better in cases when the given two bottoms b_j and b_k both seem to be visually compatible to the top t_i. Nevertheless, the general knowledge rules may also lead to the failed triplets, which could be explained by the fact that not all knowledge rules in fashion domain can be universally applicable to all the fashion item pairs.

Table 4.2: Performance comparison among different approaches in terms of AUC

Approach	AUC
POP	0.4206
RAND	0.5094
IBR	0.6075
ExIBR	0.7033
BPR-DAE	0.7616
DBPR	0.7704
AKD-DBPR-p	0.7843
AKD-DBPR-q	0.7852

Moreover, to get a deep understanding of the rule guidance, we further conducted experiments on each rule. Table 4.3 exhibits the performance of the student network and teacher network with different rules. Notably, we found that the negative rules (e.g., "no T-shirt + dress") seem to achieve better performance as compared to the positive ones (e.g., "coat + dress"). One possible explanation is that people are more likely to distinguish the incompatible pairs than the compatible ones. In addition, as we can see, rules regarding category show superiority over rules pertaining to other attributes, such as material and color. This may be due to two reasons: (1) the category related rules are more specific and acceptable by the public, and hence have strong rule confidences and provide better guidance to the neural networks and (2) the category metadata is better structured, cleaner, and more complete as compared to the loose and noisy title description, where we derived the other attributes (e.g., material and color) for fashion items. Moreover, as to the color-related rules, we found that the rule "black + black" surprisingly out-

AKD-DBPR ✓			DBPR ✗			AKD-DBPR ✗		DBPR ✓
t_i	b_j	b_k	t_i	b_j	b_k	t_i	b_j	b_k
Khaki Floral Embroidered Bomber Jacket	Floral Print Midi Dress	Skinny Jeans	White Sweatshirt	Black Plaid Mini Skirt	Printed Brocade Shorts	White Crop T-shirt	Striped Wide-Let Trousers	Black Leather Fitted Skirt
Yoins Letter Pattern Pullover Sweatshirt	Yoins Skinny Ripped Jeans in Blue	H&M Jersey Skirt	Silk Top	Tory Burch Skirt	Elastic-Waist Mini Knit Skirt	Unreal Fur Coats	Hobbs Pants	Cocktail Dresses

Figure 4.5: Comparison between AKD-DBPR and DBPR on testing triplets. All the triplets satisfy that $t_i : b_j \succ b_k$. We only list the keywords of the metadata of items and highlight the values of the rule.

performs the rule "white + black." One plausible explanation is that white tops are more versatile than black ones, suit more bottoms with different colors, and hence deteriorate the confidence of the rule "white + black." Last but not least, interestingly, we noted that the rule pertaining to the brand (i.e., Yoins) of fashion items can achieve remarkable performance. This may be due to that items of the same brand can share the brand exclusive features and hence are more likely to make suitable outfits.

4.4.3 ON ATTENTION MECHANISM (RQ2)

To evaluate the importance of the attention mechanism in the knowledge distillation, we further compared AKD-DBPR with its derivation UKD-DBPR, where the rule confidence is assigned uniformly. Moreover, to obtain a thorough understanding, we conducted the comparative experiments with different modality configurations. Table 4.4 shows the effects of the attention mechanism in our model with different modality combinations. First, as can be seen, our model consistently shows superiority over UKD-DBPR across different modality configurations, which enables us to safely draw the conclusion that it is advisable to assign rule confidence attentively rather than uniformly. Second, we observed that AKD-DBPR remarkably outperforms DBPR with only the visual modality (the relative improvement reaches 6.97%). This may be due to the fact that in this context, AKD-DBPR is able to take advantage of the contextual information to determine whether a sample satisfy the given rule, perform the knowledge distillation and hence significantly boost the performance of that solely with visual information. Moreover, we found that even with only the contextual modality, AKD-DBPR can achieve better performance than DBPR (the relative improvement is 2.69%). One possible explanation is

Table 4.3: Effects of the rule guidance. The first row refers to the performance of the baseline DBPR

ID	Top	Bottom	AUC-p	AUC-q
0	-	-	0.7704	-
1	Stripe	Stripe	0.7738	0.7738
2	Floral	Floral	0.7744	0.7739
3	White	Black	0.7714	0.7714
4	Black	Black	0.7755	0.7770
5	Cashmere	Leather	0.7770	0.7773
6	Yoins	Yoins	0.7792	0.7790
7	Tank Tops	Shorts	0.7732	0.7725
8	Sweatshirt	Activewear pants	0.7757	0.7777
9	Coat	Dress	0.7794	0.7792
10	No silk	Knit	0.7739	0.7739
11	No silk	Chiffon	0.7744	0.7744
12	No coat	Shorts	0.7760	0.7755
13	No jacket	Shorts	0.7779	0.7779
14	No blouses	Dress	0.7814	0.7814
15	No T-shirt	Dress	0.7810	0.7815

Table 4.4: Effects of the attention mechanism

Approach	Context	Visual	All
AKD-DBPR-q	0.7374	0.7302	0.7852
AKD-DBPR-p	0.7345	0.6961	0.7843
UKD-DBPR-q	0.7245	0.7280	0.7760
UKD-DBPR-p	0.7275	0.6865	0.7785
DBPR	0.7181	0.6826	0.7704

that the pure data-driven neural networks cannot accurately capture all the underlying matching rules with the limited labeled samples and thus need the domain knowledge to overcome this limitation.

Apart from the quantitative analysis, we also provided certain intuitive examples to illustrate the effects of the attention mechanism in our scheme. Figure 4.6 illustrates several examples regarding the rule confidence learned by the attention mechanism. As can be seen, different levels of rule confidence can be assigned for the same rule ("no silk + knit") with different triplets. In addition, we found that the rules pertaining to the category are usually assigned higher confidence levels. This may be attributed to that people tend to put the category attribute at the first place when they make outfits compared to other attributes. Furthermore, we also noted that although the contextual metadata indicates that the third triplet activates the rule "stripe + stripe," the learned rule confidence is not much high. This may be due to the fact that the given rule is a bit fuzzy and general and the visual signals imply the incompatibility between the stripes in the given top i and bottom k. Accordingly, to certain extent, the attention mechanism can be helpful to overcome the limitation of the human-defined fuzzy rules.

Figure 4.6: Illustration of attentive rule confidences.

4.4.4   ON FASHION ITEM RETRIEVAL (RQ3)

To assess the practical value of our work, we evaluated the proposed AKD-DBPR toward the complementary fashion item retrieval. As it is time-consuming to rank all the bottoms for each top, we adopted the common strategy [37] that feeds each top t_i appeared in S_{test} as a query, and randomly selected T bottoms as the ranking candidates, where there is only one positive bottom. Thereafter, by passing them to the trained neural networks, getting their latent representations and calculating the compatibility score m_{ij} according to Eq. (4.2), we generated a ranking list of these bottoms for the given top. In our setting, we focused on the average position of the positive bottom in the ranking list and thus adopted the MRR metric [52, 129, 135].

In total, we have 1,954 unique tops in the testing set. Due to the sparsity of the real-world dataset, we found there are 1,262 (64.59%) tops never appeared in S_{train}. To comprehensively evaluate the proposed model, we compared it with different models using different type of testing tops: observed testing tops and unobserved ones. As can be seen from Figure 4.7, AKD-DBPR and DBPR outperform all the other baselines consistently at different numbers of bottom candidates in all scenarios, which demonstrates the effectiveness of our models in complementary fashion item retrieval. In addition, AKD-DBPR and DBPR achieve satisfactory performance with both observed and unobserved tops, which validates their capability of handling the cold start problem. Last but not least, we found that AKD-DBPR outperforms DBPR in both scenarios, especially with observed testing tops, which reconfirms the importance of incorporating the domain knowledge. To have an intuitive understanding of the results, we provided certain intuitive ranking results of AKD-DBPR and DBPR for testing tops in Figure 4.8. The bottoms highlighted in the red boxes are the positive ones. By checking the context of each example, we found that they both activate certain matching rules, such as "floral + floral," "coat + dress," and "white + black," which may contribute to the good performance of AKD-DBPR.

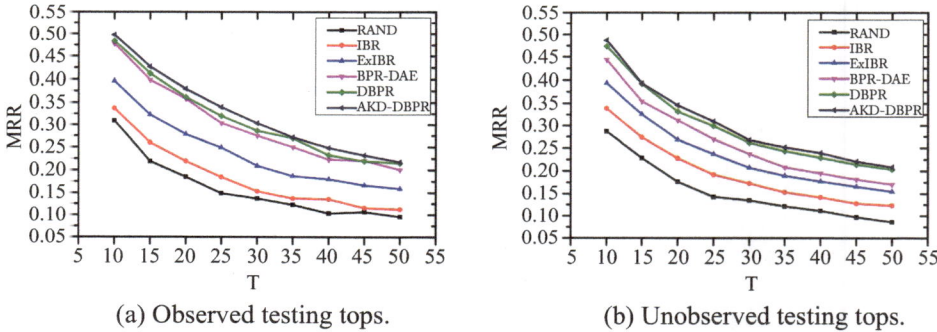

(a) Observed testing tops.   (b) Unobserved testing tops.

Figure 4.7: Performance of different models.

4.5   SUMMARY

In this chapter, we present an attentive knowledge distillation scheme toward compatibility modeling in the context of clothing matching, which jointly learns from both the specific data samples and general knowledge rules. Considering that different rules can have different confidence levels to different samples, we seamlessly sew up the attention mechanism into the knowledge distillation framework to attentively assign the rule confidence. Extensive experiments have been conducted on the real-world Dataset I and the encouraging empirical results demonstrate the effectiveness of the proposed scheme and indicate the benefits of taking the domain knowledge into consideration in the context of compatibility modeling. We found that the negative

Figure 4.8: Ranking result illustration of AKD-DBPR and DBPR. The bottoms highlighted in the red boxes are the positive ones. The first example activates the rules "floral + floral" and "coat + dress," while the second one triggers the rule "white + black."

matching rules and category related rules seem to be more powerful than others. We also exhibited the benefits of incorporating the attention mechanism into the knowledge distillation framework. One limitation of our work is that currently we only rely on the contextual metadata to identify the rules activated by the given sample, which is largely constrained by the incomplete and noisy description.

CHAPTER 5

Prototype-Wise Interpretable Compatibility Modeling

5.1 INTRODUCTION

In Chapter 4, we studied the knowledge-guided compatibility modeling, which can integrate the domain knowledge to boost the model performance and enhance the model interpretability to some extent. Nevertheless, in reality, people are more frequently faced by the following three essentially correlated questions in clothing matching. As shown in Figure 5.1, **Q1**: Are the given fashion items compatible? **Q2**: What are the discordant components that result in the incompatible matching? **Q3**: What are the alternative items to transform the incompatible pairs to compatible ones? In light of this, this chapter proposes the prototype-wise interpretable compatibility modeling, which can answer all the above questions and comprehensively facilitate people in clothing matching.

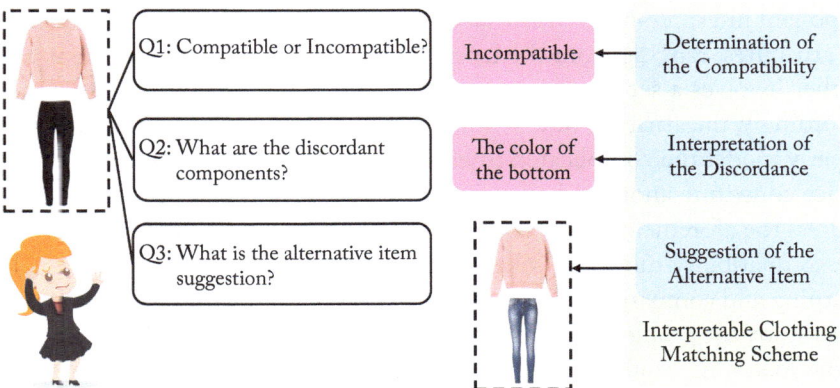

Figure 5.1: Illustration of the task.

Due to the huge success of deep learning methods in various domains, most of existing efforts employ them to learn effective representations of fashion items, based on that they can measure the compatibility between fashion items. Nevertheless, as pure data-driven learning schemes, deep learning methods suffer from the poor interpretability given that each dimension of the learned representation cannot explicitly refer to an intuitive semantic aspect of fashion items, causing questions **Q2** and **Q3** that require more result interpretations largely untapped. Notably, although a few pioneer researchers have attempted to tackle question **Q2** by enhancing the interpretability through modeling the attribute-level (e.g., *color* and *texture*) compatibility between fashion items [24], they cannot provide the comprehensive interpretation due to the extremely limited attributes they adopt.

In this work, we aim to comprehensively tackle all three of the essential problems, namely, the compatibility determination between fashion items, discordant component interpretation for incompatible outfits, and alternative item suggestion for making compatible ones. We focus on devising a versatile attribute-wise interpretable clothing matching scheme, since attributes are the most intuitive semantic cues to characterize fashion items. However, fulfilling the task in the attribute-wise manner is non-trivial due to the following challenges: (1) as aforementioned, attribute plays a pivotal role in both characterizing fashion items and interpreting the matching results. However, most existing benchmark datasets pertaining to clothing matching lack the attribute ground truth for fashion items. How to acquire the accurate fine-grained attribute representations for the benchmark datasets poses a primary challenge for us; (2) as the saying goes, birds of a feather flock together. Compatible fashion items may essentially follow certain underlying harmonious attribute interaction prototypes, while the incompatible ones would also share several unfavorable attribute compositions. For example, {*chiffon, pear-shaped, garden, beadings*} tends to be a harmonious attribute interaction prototype, while {*boyfriend-style, silk lace gauze, active wear, floral printing*} can be an incompatible one. Therefore, how to explore the latent compatible/incompatible attribute interaction prototypes and hence facilitate the discordant component interpretation is a crucial challenge; and (3) fashion items can be featured by a number of attributes, ranging from the length of trousers to the collar of the top, where each attribute further involves a set of attribute values (e.g., *long, short*, and *mini* for the length attribute). Accordingly, the attribute interaction between fashion items can be rather complicated. How to properly model the complicated interactions among various attributes and distinguish the discordance constitute another challenge.

To address the aforementioned challenges, we propose a prototype-guided attribute-wise interpretable compatibility modeling scheme, termed PAICM, to jointly regularize the latent prototype learning and compatibility modeling, as shown in Figure 5.2. Without losing the generality, here we study the problem of clothing matching between tops and bottoms. In particular, to facilitate the matching result interpretation, the scheme first extracts the semantic attribute representations for fashion items with a set of advanced neural networks, where each network is aligned to an attribute to ensure the quality of the attribute representation. Notably, to enhance the portability of PAICM, apart from our primary dataset adopted for clothing matching, we introduce an auxiliary dataset of fashion items with rich attribute annotations to pre-train the attribute classification networks. Based on the learned attribute representations, on one hand, the proposed scheme explores the latent compatible and incompatible attribute interaction prototypes using the non-negative matrix factorization (NMF) [65]. The learned prototypes are

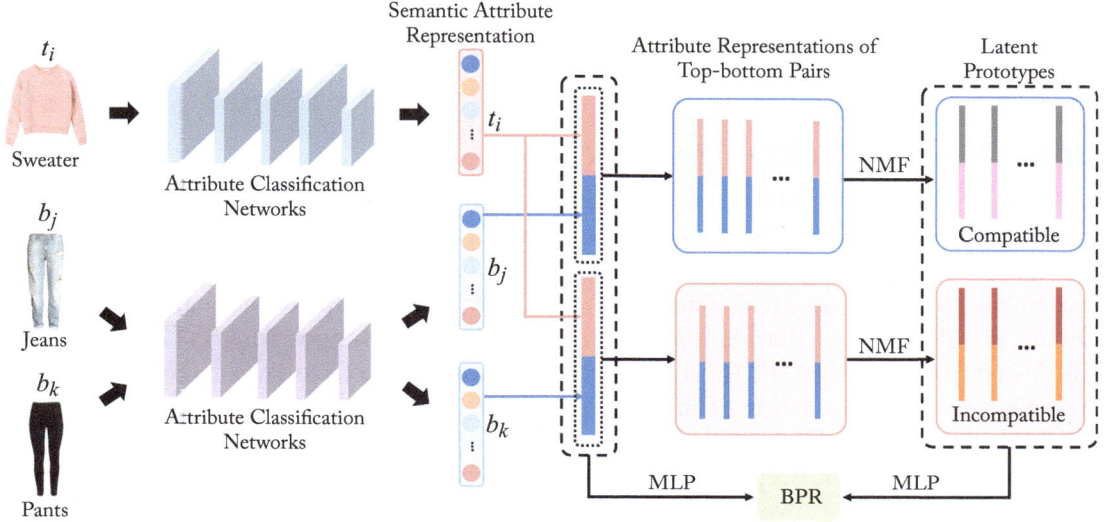

Figure 5.2: Illustration of the proposed scheme. We obtain the semantic attribute representations via the pre-trained attribute classification network, based on which we employ the NMF framework to explore the latent compatible and incompatible prototypes. We jointly regularize the latent prototype learning and compatibility modeling with the BPR framework.

regarded as the templates to guide the discordant attribute interpretation and the alternative item suggestion. On the other hand, toward compatibility modeling, the proposed scheme seeks the latent space to accurately measure the compatibility between fashion items using the MLP. Ultimately, the proposed scheme seamlessly integrates the latent prototype learning and compatibility modeling with the BPR framework [100], where the pairwise preferences between attribute prototypes and fashion items can be adaptively coupled and well exploited.

5.2   RELATED WORK

5.2.1   INTERPRETABLE COMPATIBILITY MODELING

As mentioned in Chapters 3 and 4, although existing studies [31, 67, 69, 86, 108] have achieved compelling success in fashion analysis, especially the compatibility modeling, they mainly focused on utilizing deep learning methods to represent fashion items with the blurry semantic features, resulting in their poor interpretability. To enhance the model interpretability, Feng et. al. [24] proposed a partition embedding network to learn the embedding of each attribute and then model the attribute-level compatibility between fashion items. Despite the promising performance it accomplished, the attributes regarding the compatibility of fashion items can be numerous yet they only adopted limited ones, making the interpretation incomprehensive.

Distinguished from these studies, we aim to not only improve the interpretability of the clothing matching in a comprehensive attribute-wise manner but also facilitate the alternative item suggestion.

5.2.2   MATRIX FACTORIZATION

As a numerical analysis method, matrix factorization (MF) is widely applied in various research areas, such as the item recommendation [36, 61, 114, 121] and information retrieval [79, 97, 113], due to its superior performance in discovering the latent features between two entities (e.g., the user and item). In order to effectively adapt to different tasks, several variants of MF have been devised, such as the singular value decomposition (SVD) [17], probabilistic matrix factorization (PMF) [89], and non-negative matrix factorization (NMF) [65], and their efficiency has been validated in various domains. For example, Sun et al. [111] proposed a SVDNet to fulfill the retrieval task of person re-identification (reID), where the SVD is employed to optimize of the deep representation learning process. In addition, Kim et al. [56] presented a context-aware convolutional matrix factorization (ConvMF) that integrates the CNN into the PMF in the context of document context-aware recommendation. Besides, as a useful tool for the sparse and meaningful feature extraction, NMF also drew researchers' attentions. For example, Xu et al. [124] proposed a document clustering method based on the NMF with the term-document matrix. Furthermore, to forecast the fashion styles, Ziad et. al. [139] employed the NMF to discover the latent clothing styles in an unsupervised manner. Although the NMF has been successfully applied to solve tasks like text clustering [124], fashion trending prediction [139], and recommender systems [2], limited efforts have been dedicated to the complementary clothing matching, which is the major concern of our work.

5.3   METHODOLOGY

In this section, we first formally give the research problem formulation, and then detail the proposed PAICM.

5.3.1   PROBLEM FORMULATION

In the real-world clothing matching scenarios, users may not only want to know whether the given fashion items are compatible or not, but also expect to get advice on how to harmonize the improper outfit. In this context, we aim to devise an attribute-wise interpretable compatibility modeling scheme to explain the underlying reasons why the given items are incompatible in the attribute-wise manner and provide the potential attribute manipulations to make compatible outfits. Suppose that we have a set of tops $\mathcal{T} = \{t_1, t_2, \ldots, t_{N_t}\}$ and bottoms $\mathcal{B} = \{b_1, b_2, \ldots, b_{N_b}\}$, where N_t and N_b denote the total number of tops and bottoms, respectively. In this work, we characterize each fashion item with a set of attributes (e.g., the *color* and *category*) $\mathcal{A} = \{a_q\}_{q=1}^{Q}$, where a_q is the q-th attribute and Q is the total number of attributes. Each attribute a_q is associated with a set of elements representing its possible values $\mathcal{E}_q = \{e_q^1, e_q^2, \ldots, e_q^{M_q}\}$, where e_q^i refers to the i-th element and M_q is the total number of elements regarding a_q. For simplicity, we compile all $\mathcal{E}_q$'s in order and hence derive a unified set of attribute elements $\mathcal{E} = \bigcup_{q=1}^{Q} \mathcal{E}_q = \{e_1, e_2, \ldots, e_M\}$, where $M = \sum_{q=1}^{Q} M_q$. In addition, we have a set of positive top-bottom pairs $\mathcal{S} = \{(t_{i_1}, b_{j_1}), (t_{i_2}, b_{j_2}), \ldots, (t_{i_N}, b_{j_N})\}$ composed by fashion experts, where N is the total number of positive pairs. Accordingly, for each top t_i, we can derive a set of positive bottoms $\mathcal{B}_i^+ = \{b_j \in \mathcal{B}|(t_i, b_j) \in \mathcal{S}\}$. Let s_{ij} denote the compatibility between the top t_i and bottom b_j, based on which we can distinguish whether the given fashion items are compatible or not.

5.3.2   SEMANTIC ATTRIBUTE REPRESENTATION

As a matter of fact, the online fashion item is usually characterized by a visual image, certain user-generated contextual description and structured category labels. In a sense, the visual image and structured category labels can faithfully capture the essential features of fashion items, such as the *color*, *shape*, and *category*, while the user-generated contextual description may be unreliable as it can be intrinsically noisy, not to mention the mendacious ones edited by crafty sellers. Therefore, similar to the existing work [139], we only exploit the reliable visual cues as well as the structured category information to model the compatibility between fashion items. Notably, existing efforts mainly adopt advanced deep neural networks to learn the effective presentations for fashion items and measure the compatibility owing to their compelling success in various research tasks. Nevertheless, as a pure data-driven learning scheme, deep neural network suffers from the poor interpretability due to the fact that each dimension of the learned representation cannot explicitly refer to the intuitive semantic aspect of fashion items. Toward this end, we aim to learn the meaningful representations for fashion items, whose dimensions directly stand for the semantic attributes and hence enhance the model interpretability.

On one hand, regarding the sophisticated visual signals, we argue that taking advantage of the well pre-trained attribute classification networks is the most natural and straightforward way to obtain the interpretable semantic representations of fashion items. As to ensure the performance of the attribute classification networks, we align each attribute a_q with a separate attribute classification network h_q. It is worth noting that as the category information also contributes an essential attribute of fashion items, here we have $Q - 1$ attributes characterized by the visual cues. We feed the visual image $\mathbf{I}_i$ of the i-th top/bottom into these h_q's, and obtain the semantic attribute representations as follows:

$$\mathbf{f}_i^q = h_q\left(\mathbf{I}_i | \mathbf{\Theta}_q\right), \quad q = 1, 2, \ldots, Q - 1, \tag{5.1}$$

where $\mathbf{\Theta}_q$ denotes the network parameter of h_q and $\mathbf{f}_i^q \in \mathbb{R}^{M_q}$ is the network output of h_q. The d-th entry in $\mathbf{f}_i^q$ refers to the probability that the top t_i presents the attribute element e_q^d. In particular, we denote $\mathbf{f}_i^v = [\mathbf{f}_i^1; \mathbf{f}_i^2; \ldots; \mathbf{f}_i^{Q-1}]$ as the final semantic attribute representation of the

i-th top/bottom derived from the visual signals, where ";" is the cascading operation of vectors in the vertical direction.

On the other hand, the intuitive nature of the structured category information propels us to encode it directly with the one-hot representation. Let $\mathbf{f}_i^c$ stands for the one-hot semantic attribute representation derived from the category context for the i-th top/bottom. Ultimately, we concatenate the attribute representations obtained from both sources and generate the final semantic attribute representation $\mathbf{f}_i = [\mathbf{f}_i^v; \mathbf{f}_i^c]$ for the i-th item.

5.3.3   LATENT COMPATIBILITY SPACE

Apparently, it is not advisable to directly measure the compatibility in the raw attribute space. Similar to our previous work [109], we assume that there is a latent compatibility space that enables us to accurately model the complicated attribute interactions and hence boost the compatibility modeling performance. In this chapter, we resort to the MLP, which has shown superior performance in various representation learning tasks [73–75, 120]. In particular, we add K hidden layers over the semantic attribute representation of the fashion item as follows:

$$
\begin{cases}
\mathbf{f}_{i0}^y = \mathbf{f}_i^y, \\
\mathbf{f}_{ik}^y = \sigma\left(\mathbf{W}_k^y \mathbf{f}_{i(k-1)}^y + \mathbf{b}_k^y\right), \quad k = 1, \ldots, K, \quad y \in \{t, b\},
\end{cases}
\tag{5.2}
$$

where $\mathbf{f}_{ik}^y$ is the k-th layer hidden representation, $\mathbf{W}_k^y$ and $\mathbf{b}_k^y$ are weight matrices and biases, respectively. t and b denote *top* and *bottom*, respectively. $\sigma : \mathbb{R} \mapsto \mathbb{R}$ is a nonlinear function applied in an element-wise manner, where we choose the sigmoid function $\sigma(x) = \frac{1}{1+e^{-x}}$ in this work. The latent representation of the fashion item is defined as the output of the K-th layer, i.e., $\tilde{\mathbf{f}}_i^y = \mathbf{f}_{iK}^y \in \mathbb{R}^{D_l}$, $y \in \{t, b\}$, where D_l denotes the dimension of the latent compatibility space. Therefore, the compatibility between top t_i and bottom b_j can be measured as follows:

$$
s_{ij} = \left(\tilde{\mathbf{f}}_i^t\right)^T \tilde{\mathbf{f}}_j^b.
\tag{5.3}
$$

Adopting the BPR framework for its excellent performance on the implicit preference modeling [6, 36], we first construct the training set $\mathcal{D}_S := \{(i, j, k) | t_i \in \mathcal{T}, b_j \in \mathcal{B}_i^+ \wedge b_k \in \mathcal{B} \setminus \mathcal{B}_i^+\}$, where the triplet (i, j, k) indicates that top t_i goes better with bottom b_j as compared with bottom b_k. Then according to [100], the objective function can be written as follows:

$$
\mathcal{L}_{bpr}^{item} = \sum_{(i,j,k)\in\mathcal{D}_S} -\ln\left(\sigma\left(s_{ij} - s_{ik}\right)\right) + \frac{\lambda}{2}\|\mathbf{\Omega}\|_F^2,
\tag{5.4}
$$

where σ is the sigmoid function, λ is the non-negative hyperparameter to avoid the overfitting, and $\mathbf{\Omega}$ denotes the set of parameters (i.e., $\mathbf{W}_k^y$'s and $\mathbf{b}_k^y$'s).

5.3.4 PROTOTYPE-GUIDED COMPATIBILITY MODELING

Intuitively, compatible fashion items can essentially follow several latent compatible attribute interaction prototypes, while the incompatible ones would share certain unfavorable prototypes. In a sense, each latent prototype can be characterized by a set of attribute elements. For example, {*jeans, boyfriend-style, ragged, street fashion*} tends to form a harmonious prototype, while {*office lady, holed, cartoon, tiered skirt*} is more likely to refer to an unfavorable one. Toward this end, we assume that there is a set of latent compatible/incompatible attribute interaction prototypes.

Owing to its superior capability of latent factor modeling [66], we seek the latent attribute interaction prototypes under the NMF. To derive the latent attribute interaction compatible prototypes, it is natural to resort to the set of positive top-bottom pairs $\mathcal{S}$. Here we define the data matrix $\mathbf{G}_p = [\mathbf{g}_1, \mathbf{g}_2, \ldots, \mathbf{g}_N] \in \mathbb{R}^{2M \times N}$, where $\mathbf{g}_n = [\mathbf{f}_{i_n}^t; \mathbf{f}_{j_n}^b] \in \mathbb{R}^{2M}$ denotes the semantic attribute representation of the n-th positive top-bottom pair (t_{i_n}, b_{j_n}).

According to NMF, we aim to solve the following objective:

$$\min_{\mathbf{P}, \mathbf{H}_p} \left\| \mathbf{G}_p - \mathbf{P}\mathbf{H}_p \right\|_F^2 ,$$
$$\text{s.t. } \mathbf{P} \geqslant 0, \mathbf{H}_p \geqslant 0, \tag{5.5}$$

where $\mathbf{P} = [\mathbf{p}_1, \mathbf{p}_2, \cdots, \mathbf{p}_{L_p}] \in \mathbb{R}^{2M \times L_p}$ refers to the latent basis matrix, each column of which corresponds to a compatible prototype, and L_p represents the total number of the latent prototypes. $\mathbf{H}_p \in \mathbb{R}^{L_p \times N}$ corresponds to the latent representation matrix of the N top-bottom pairs regarding the basis compatibility prototypes. In particular, $\mathbf{p}_l \in \mathbb{R}^{2M}$ denotes the l-th latent compatible prototype, which can be rewritten as follows:

$$\mathbf{p}_l = \begin{bmatrix} \mathbf{p}_l^t \\ \mathbf{p}_l^b \end{bmatrix}, \tag{5.6}$$

where $\mathbf{p}_l^t \in \mathbb{R}^M$ and $\mathbf{p}_l^b \in \mathbb{R}^M$ can be treated as the semantic attribute representations of the prototype top and bottom for $\mathbf{p}_l$.

In the same manner, we can also derive the latent incompatible prototypes based on the set of negative top-bottom pairs (t_i, b_k)'s, where the bottom $b_k \notin \mathcal{B}_i^+$ is randomly sampled for top t_i. Let $\mathbf{G}_u \in \mathbb{R}^{2M \times N}$ be the data matrix comprising semantic attribute representations of negative top-bottom pairs and $\mathbf{U} = [\mathbf{u}_1, \mathbf{u}_2, \cdots, \mathbf{u}_{L_u}] \in \mathbb{R}^{2M \times L_u}$ be the matrix of latent incompatible prototypes, where L_u is the total number of incompatible prototypes, and $\mathbf{H}_u \in \mathbb{R}^{L_u \times N}$ denotes the latent representation matrix of the N negative top-bottom pairs in the prototype space. Similarly, we represent the r-th latent incompatible prototype $\mathbf{u}_r \in \mathbb{R}^{2M}$ as follows:

$$\mathbf{u}_r = \begin{bmatrix} \mathbf{u}_r^t \\ \mathbf{u}_r^b \end{bmatrix}, \tag{5.7}$$

where $\mathbf{u}_r^t \in \mathbb{R}^M$ and $\mathbf{u}_r^b \in \mathbb{R}^M$ denote the semantic attribute representations of the prototype top and bottom of $\mathbf{u}_r$. Ultimately, we have the following NMF loss for the latent prototype learning,

$$\mathcal{L}_{nmf} = \left\| \mathbf{G}_p - \mathbf{PH}_p \right\|_F^2 + \left\| \mathbf{G}_u - \mathbf{UH}_u \right\|_F^2 . \tag{5.8}$$

It is intuitive that the top and bottom of one compatible prototype should be more compatible than those of the incompatible ones. Therefore, we define the intrinsic compatibility for each prototype $\mathbf{p}_l$ $(\mathbf{u}_r)$ as follows:

$$s_l^p = \left(\tilde{\mathbf{p}}_l^t \right)^T \tilde{\mathbf{p}}_l^b, \qquad s_r^u = \left(\tilde{\mathbf{u}}_r^t \right)^T \tilde{\mathbf{u}}_r^b, \tag{5.9}$$

where s_l^p and s_r^u are the intrinsic compatibility for the compatible prototype $\mathbf{p}_l$ and incompatible prototype $\mathbf{u}_r$, respectively. $\tilde{\mathbf{p}}_l^t$, $\tilde{\mathbf{p}}_l^b$, $\tilde{\mathbf{u}}_r^t$, and $\tilde{\mathbf{u}}_r^b$ are the hidden representations of $\mathbf{p}_l^t$, $\mathbf{p}_l^b$, $\mathbf{u}_r^t$, and $\mathbf{u}_r^b$, respectively, which can be acquired based on Eq. (5.2).

To seamlessly integrate the latent prototype learning and compatible modeling, for each sample (i, j, k), we particularly define its most similar compatible and incompatible prototypes $\mathbf{p}_{l*}$ and $\mathbf{u}_{r*}$ with the Euclidean distance, whose indexes l^* and r^* can be derived as follows:

$$\begin{cases} d_p(i, j, l) = \left\| \begin{bmatrix} \mathbf{f}_i^t \\ \mathbf{f}_j^b \end{bmatrix} - \begin{bmatrix} \mathbf{p}_l^t \\ \mathbf{p}_l^b \end{bmatrix} \right\|_2, \; d_u(i, k, r) = \left\| \begin{bmatrix} \mathbf{f}_i^t \\ \mathbf{f}_k^b \end{bmatrix} - \begin{bmatrix} \mathbf{u}_r^t \\ \mathbf{u}_r^b \end{bmatrix} \right\|_2, \\ l^* = \arg\min_l d_p(i, j, l) \qquad , \quad r^* = \arg\min_r d_u(i, k, r). \end{cases} \tag{5.10}$$

In a sense, we expect that the intrinsic compatibility of the compatible prototype $\mathbf{p}_{l*}$ should be higher than that of the incompatible one $\mathbf{u}_{r*}$. Therefore according to the BPR, we thus have the following adaptive objective function:

$$\mathcal{L}_{bpr}^{proto} = \sum_{(i,j,k) \in \mathcal{D}_S} -\ln \left(\sigma \left(s_{l*}^p - s_{r*}^u \right) \right), \tag{5.11}$$

where s_{l*}^p and s_{r*}^u can be obtained with Eq. (5.9). Interestingly, with $\mathcal{L}_{bpr}^{item}$ and $\mathcal{L}_{bpr}^{proto}$, the compatibility modeling between fashion items and the prototype learning can be mutually promoted. Ultimately, we obtain the final objective function as follows:

$$\mathcal{L} = \mathcal{L}_{bpr}^{item} + \mu \mathcal{L}_{bpr}^{proto} + \upsilon \mathcal{L}_{nmf}, \tag{5.12}$$

where μ and υ are the non-negative trade-off hyperparameters to weigh the different components of the objective function.

5.3.5   INTERPRETABLE ATTRIBUTE MANIPULATION

In order to transform the incompatible fashion item pairs into the compatible ones, we first employ the L_p compatible prototypes as templates to identify the discordant attributes. In particular, for the given negative (incompatible) top-bottom pair (t_i, b_k), we particularly find the most similar compatible prototype $\mathbf{p}_{l*}$ according to Eq. (5.10). For simplicity, we divide $\mathbf{p}_{l*}$ into Z parts as follows:

$$\mathbf{p}_{l*} = \left[\mathbf{p}_{l*}^1; \ldots; \mathbf{p}_{l*}^Q; \mathbf{p}_{l*}^{Q+1}; \ldots; \mathbf{p}_{l*}^Z \right], \tag{5.13}$$

where $Z = 2Q$. The first Q parts refer to the attribute representations of the top in prototype $\mathbf{p}_{l*}$, while the last Q parts correspond to that of the bottom in $\mathbf{p}_{l*}$. In the same manner, the negative top-bottom pair (t_i, b_k) can be represented as follows:

$$\mathbf{g}_{ik} = \left[\mathbf{f}_i^t; \mathbf{f}_k^b \right] = \left[\mathbf{g}_{ik}^1; \ldots; \mathbf{g}_{ik}^Q; \mathbf{g}_{ik}^{Q+1}; \ldots; \mathbf{g}_{ik}^Z \right]. \tag{5.14}$$

Moreover, we define the attribute-wise difference between (t_i, b_k) and $\mathbf{p}_{l*}$ as follows:

$$d_e\left(i, k, l^*, z\right) = \frac{\left\| \mathbf{g}_{ik}^z - \mathbf{p}_{l*}^z \right\|_2}{M_z}, \tag{5.15}$$

where $d_e(i, k, l^*, z)$ denotes the attribute difference between (t_i, b_k) and $\mathbf{p}_{l*}$ regarding the z-th attribute. We then identify the most discordant attribute that causes the incompatibility as follows:

$$z^* = \arg\max_z d_e(i, k, l^*, z). \tag{5.16}$$

Thereafter, to suggest the alternative item and make the compatible pair, we replace the attribute representation $\mathbf{g}_{ik}^{z^*}$ of (t_i, b_k) with $\mathbf{p}_{l*}^{z^*}$ and hence obtain the manipulated semantic attribute representation as follows:

$$\hat{\mathbf{g}}_{ik} = \begin{cases} \left[\hat{\mathbf{f}}_i^t; \mathbf{f}_k^b \right], \text{if } z^* \leq Q, \\ \left[\mathbf{f}_i^t; \hat{\mathbf{f}}_k^b \right], \text{if } z^* > Q, \end{cases} \tag{5.17}$$

where $\hat{\mathbf{f}}_i^t$ and $\hat{\mathbf{f}}_k^b$ are the manipulated semantic attribute representations of top t_i and bottom b_k, respectively, with which we can retrieve the new fashion items to make a compatible matching. In particular, if the discordant attribute manipulation needs to be taken on the top t_i (i.e., $z^* \leq Q$), we can retrieve new tops $t_{i'}$'s by ranking the Euclidean distance d_p's between $\hat{\mathbf{f}}_i^t$ and the semantic attribute representations of training tops in the decent order. Otherwise, we can retrieve new bottoms $b_{k'}$'s by ranking d_p's between $\hat{\mathbf{f}}_k^b$ and the representations of training bottoms. The workflow of attribute manipulation is shown in Figure 5.3, and the algorithm of the proposed method is summarized in Algorithm 5.2.

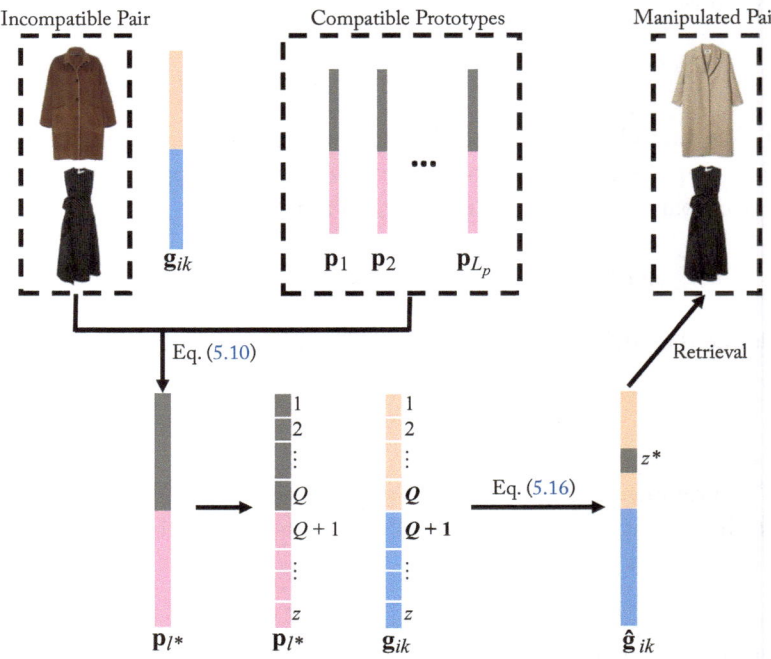

Figure 5.3: Illustration of the workflow of attribute manipulation.

Algorithm 5.2 Interpretable Clothing Matching and Retrieval.

Input: $\mathcal{D}_S = \{(i, j, k)\}, \mu, \lambda, L_p, L_n$
Output: Parameters Ω in MLP, parameters $\mathbf{P}$, $\mathbf{H}$, and $\mathbf{U}$ in NMF.
1: Initialize neural network parameters in MLP and NMF.
2: **repeat**
3:    Randomly draw (i, j, k) from $\mathcal{D}_S$
4:    Calculate l^* and r^* according to Eq. (5.10).
5:    Update Θ and Φ according to Eq. (5.12).
6: **until** Converge
7: Calculate the incompatible attribute in the negative top-bottom pair according to Eq. (5.16)
8: Manipulate the incompatible attribute to get the new semantic attribute representation and retrieve the new fashion item.

5.4   EXPERIMENT

To validate the effectiveness of the proposed model, we conducted extensive experiments on the real-world Dataset I by answering the following questions.

- Does our PAICM outperform the state-of-the-art methods?

- What is the effect of NMF in the prototype-guided attribute manipulation?

- How does the proposed PAICM perform in the complementary fashion item retrieval?

We first give the experiment settings and then present experiment results with detailed analyses on each above research question.

5.4.1   EXPERIMENT SETTINGS

Auxiliary Dataset. To evaluate our PAICM, apart from the Dataset I, we utilized an auxiliary benchmark dataset of **DeepFashion** [81] to train the attribute classification networks and obtain the semantic attribute representations of fashion items. This benchmark comprises 33,881 fashion items, each of which is labeled by 18 attributes with 303 attribute elements. Table 5.1 shows several attribute examples and the corresponding attribute elements. Due to the uneven distribution of the data, we implemented the data augmentation for certain attribute classes with limited samples by multiple operations (e.g., copy, rotation and shift) with an integrated tool of Keras.

Table 5.1: Examples of attributes and the corresponding attribute elements

Attribute	Attribute Element
Type of trousers	Harem pants, straight pants
Length of trousers	Three-quarter pants, pirate shorts
Type of clothes buttons	Single-breasted, one button
Fitness of clothes	Rectangle-shaped, hourglass-shaped
Length of dresses	Below knee, above knee
Type of dresses	A-line dress, pouf dress
Style of clothes	Forest living style, boyfriend-style
Texture of clothes	Contrast color, hollow

Attribute Representation Learning. Regarding the semantic attribute representation learning, we adopted the architecture similar to AlexNet [62] that consists of five convolutional layers followed by three fully connected layers. We randomly divided the auxiliary dataset into two chunks: training set (80%) and testing set (20%), and chose the widely used cross-entropy loss to train all the networks. We adopted the area under the ROC curve (AUC) [4] to evaluate the performance of the attribute representation learning. To gain more detailed insights, we further categorized fashion items in DeepFashion into the three groups: tops, trousers, and dresses (skirts). Table 5.2 details the classification result of each attribute, where the last row "Total" refers to the average AUC weighted by the number of attribute elements. As can be seen, the overall performance of attribute classification with respect to AUC is satisfactory. Due to the fact that the auxiliary dataset lacks the annotations for the color attribute, for each fashion item in Dataset I, we extracted the color attribute based on the histogram calculation in the HSV space and encoded it to an one-hot vector as the color representation of the fashion item.

Table 5.2: Performance of the attribute classification in terms of AUC

Attribute	Tops	Trousers	Dresses (Skirts)
Length of upper-body clothes	0.7606	-	-
Type of trousers	-	0.7233	-
Part details of clothes	0.8462	0.8697	0.8181
Type of clothes buttons	0.6742	-	-
Length of trousers	-	0.7707	-
Style of clothes	0.7698	0.7575	0.8325
Fabric of clothes	0.8117	0.8738	0.8241
Type of waistlines	-	0.8171	0.7798
Texture of clothes	0.7668	0.8170	0.7387
Graphic elements of clothes	0.7433	0.8166	0.7741
Length of dresses	-	-	0.8243
Design of dresses	-	-	0.8446
Length of sleeves	0.7975	-	-
Fitness of clothes	0.7135	-	-
Type of collars	0.7839	-	-
Type of dresses	-	-	0.7694
Thickness of clothes	0.7668	0.8126	-
Type of sleeves	0.7219	-	-
Total results	0.7873	0.8280	0.8083

Parameter Tuning. We divided the positive pair set S into two parts: the training set S_{train} (80%) and testing set S_{test} (20%). For each positive pair (t_i, b_j), we randomly sampled three bottoms b_k's ($b_k \notin \mathcal{B}_i^+$), and each b_k corresponds to a triplet (i, j, k). We adopted the

AUC [99, 133] as the evaluation metric. For optimization, we employed the stochastic gradient descent (SGD) [3]. In particular, we applied a non-negative constraint in each iteration to optimize NMF. We adopted the grid search strategy to determine the optimal values on a set of validation data temporarily split from the S_{train} for the regularization parameters (i.e., λ, μ and υ) among the values $\{10^r | r \in \{-4, \ldots, -1\}\}$, $[0.2, 0.4, 0.6, 0.8]$ and $[0.05, 0.1, 0.2, 0.3]$, respectively. In addition, the number of hidden units and learning rate are searched in $[128, 256, 512]$ and $[0.0001, 0.0005, 0.001]$, respectively. The proposed model is fine-tuned for 200 epochs, and the performance on the testing set is reported. We empirically found that the proposed model achieves the optimal performance with $K = 1$ hidden layer of 256 hidden units.

5.4.2   ON COMPARISON OF APPROACHES (RQ1)

As for the compatibility modeling, we chose the following content-based baselines to evaluate the proposed model.

- **POP**: We used the "popularity" of bottom b_j to measure its compatibility with top t_i. Here the "popularity" is defined as the number of tops that has been paired with b_j in the training set.

- **RAND**: We randomly assigned the compatibility scores of s_{ij} and s_{ik} between items.

- **Bi-LSTM**: We chose the bidirectional long short-term memory (LSTM) model in [31] which explores the outfit compatibility by sequentially predicting the next item conditioned on previous ones. In our context, we adapted Bi-LSTM to deal with an outfit comprising of a top and a bottom.

- **ExIBR**: We extended the image-based recommendation (IBR) method proposed in [86] to ExIBR to handle both the visual data and the structured category label of fashion items.

- **BPR-DAE**: We selected the content-based neural scheme introduced by [108] to jointly model the coherent relation between different modalities of fashion items and the implicit preference among items via a dual autoencoder network.

To compare all the approaches fairly, we utilized both the visual image and category metadata in Bi-LSTM, ExIBR, BPR-DAE, and PAICM. Table 5.3 shows the performance comparison among different approaches. As we can see, PAICM outperforms all the other baselines, indicating the superiority of introducing the semantic attribute representations to the compatibility modeling. One possible explanation is that the compatibility modeling task is indeed to model the complicated interactions among various attributes of fashion items, and our semantic attribute representation seems to be just task-oriented.

Moreover, as the prototype learning plays a pivotal role in our PAICM, we particularly investigate the impact of the number of the prototypes learned by the NMF on the performance of compatibility modeling. For simplicity, we adopted the same number of the compatible and

Table 5.3: Performance comparison among different approaches in terms of AUC

Approach	AUC
POP	0.4206
RAND	0.5094
BPR-DAE	0.6026
ExIBR	0.6366
PAICM	0.7130

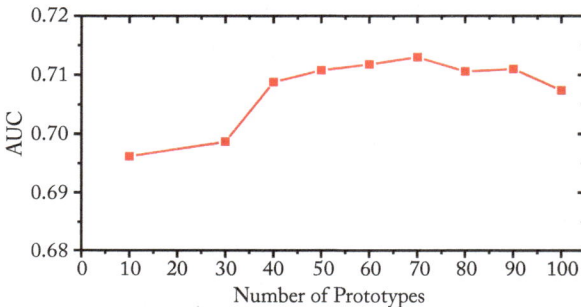

Figure 5.4: Performance of PAICM with respect to the number of prototypes.

incompatible prototypes, and varied that from 10–100 with a step of 10. Figure 5.4 shows the performance of our PAICM with different numbers of prototypes. We found that the performance is relatively steady for the number of prototypes ranging from 40–90, where 70 is the optimal number of prototypes. This suggests that our model is not much sensitive to the number of prototypes.

To obtain the deep insights, we illustrate several learned compatible and incompatible prototypes with certain intuitive top-bottom pairs in Figure 5.5, where for each prototype we list the two most similar top-bottom pairs according to Eq. (5.10). For clear illustration, we further give several notable attributes for each prototype based on their semantic representations. From Figure 5.5, we observed that the latent compatible/incompatible prototypes do share certain attribute interaction patterns. For example, "*white+black,*" "*coat+dress,*" and "*colledge+bow*" are the compatible attribute interactions while "*office lady+sweet*" and "*street fashion+slim fit*" are the incompatible ones. In addition, we noticed that the learned compatible prototypes are reasonable and compatible enough to be the guidance of the discordant attribute identification and the alternative item suggestion for incompatible top-bottom pairs.

Figure 5.5: Illustration of the compatible and incompatible prototypes. We listed some notable attributes of the prototypes according to the semantic representations of the top-bottom pair.

5.4.3   ON PROTOTYPE-GUIDED ATTRIBUTE MANIPULATION (RQ2)

To quantitatively evaluate the effects of NMF in the prototype learning, we compared NMF with K-means [32], the most commonly used unsupervised clustering method [8] that is able to group samples sharing the common characteristics. In particular, we utilized the K-means algorithm to divide our positive top-bottom pairs into L_p clusters, and the center of each cluster is treated as the learned compatible prototype. Then according to Eqs. (5.10) and (5.16), we can find the discordant attribute and replace it with the corresponding attribute representation of the most similar compatible prototype to obtain the manipulated semantic attribute representation. As our compatibility modeling scheme PAICM is able to measure the compatibility between fashion items, here we adopted the rate of the manipulated pairs with improved compatibility as the evaluation metric. Formally, the rate is defined as $|\mathcal{M}|/|\mathcal{N}|$, where $\mathcal{N}$ denotes the set of negative top-bottom pairs determined by our PAICM model and $\mathcal{M}$ refers to the set of negative pairs, whose compatibility is improved by the attribute manipulation.

Figure 5.6 illustrates the performance comparison between NMF and K-means with different numbers of compatible prototypes. As can be seen, NMF consistently surpasses K-means in all configurations, demonstrating the superiority of NMF in discovering the latent prototypes. Moreover, we found that when the number of the compatible prototype is 60, we can achieve

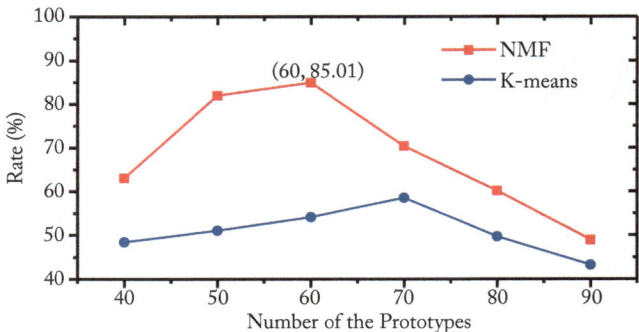

Figure 5.6: Performance comparison between the NMF and K-means respected to the rate of the manipulated pairs with improved compatibility.

the optimal performance, where 85.01% of the incompatible top-bottom pairs get the compatibility improvement after the attribute manipulation. Overall, the performance is promising and validates the effectiveness of PAICM in identifying the discordant attribute and giving the reasonable alternative item suggestion. To intuitively reflect the effect of the attribute manipulation, we illustrate several examples of the manipulated top-bottom pairs in Figure 5.7. As we can see, the slight attribute manipulation of the incompatible top-bottom pair is able to not only improve the compatibility but also preserve the original fashion styles, which can be easily accepted by people.

To comprehensively assess our model in attribute manipulation, apart from the above objective evaluation, we further conducted the subjective user study, where we invited 20 fashion-lovers to complete the psycho-visual test over 11 randomly selected incompatible top-bottom pairs. In particular, the attendees were asked to answer 11 independent questions by choosing the more compatible one between the original incompatible top-bottom pair and the manipulated one. All questions are presented twice to avoid the accident mistakes. The attendees taking part in the psychophysical experiment consists of 6 males and 14 females. The result of the psycho-visual test is shown in Table 5.4. We illustrate the maximum, minimum, and average support rates of the 11 top-bottom pairs. As we can see, overall, the fashion-lovers supported the manipulated top-bottom pairs rather than the original ones, which is consistent with the above objective evaluation result.

5.4.4   ON FASHION ITEM RETRIEVAL (RQ3)

To assess the practical value of PAICM, we conducted experiments on the complementary fashion item retrieval. Considering the fact that it is time-consuming to rank all the bottoms for each top, we utilized the same strategy in [36] to feed each top t_i appeared in S_{test} as a query, and randomly selected T bottoms as the ranking candidates with only one positive bottom. We fed

Figure 5.7: Illustration of the examples of the manipulated top-bottom pairs. The descriptions below the pairs are the manipulated incompatible attributes.

Table 5.4: Comparison among the original and manipulated top-bottom pairs by fashion lovers

Support Rate	Original	Manipulated
Average support rate	20.68%	79.32%
Maximum support rate	46.15%	100.00%
Minimum support rate	0.00%	53.58%

the candidates into the trained model to acquire their latent representations and calculated the compatibility score s_{ij} according to Eq. (5.3), based on which we generated a ranking list of the bottoms for the given top. In this work, we focused on the average position of the positive bottom in the ranking list and thus adopted the MRR metric [52, 129, 135].

In total, there are 1,954 unique tops in the testing set. Due to the sparsity of the real-world dataset, 1,262 (64.59%) tops never appear in $\mathcal{S}_{train}$. To comprehensively evaluate the proposed model, we divided tops in the testing set into two ground: observed testing tops and unobserved ones. As shown in Figure 5.8, PAICM shows superiority over all the other baselines at different

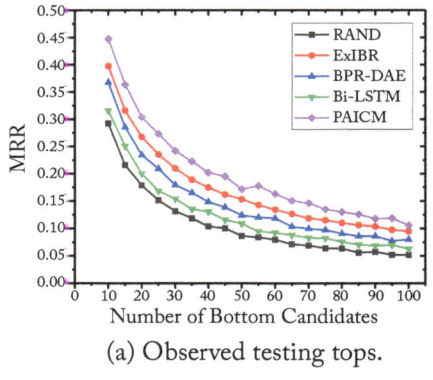

(a) Observed testing tops.

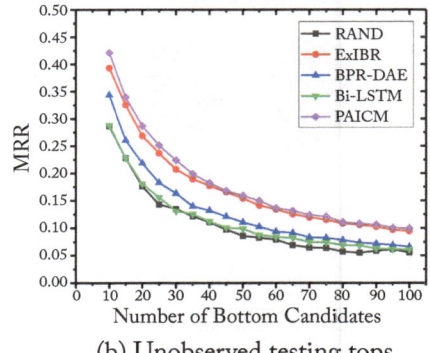

(b) Unobserved testing tops.

Figure 5.8: Performance of different models.

numbers of bottom candidates in both scenarios, indicating the robustness and effectiveness of PAICM in complementary fashion item retrieval.

5.5   SUMMARY

In this chapter, we present a prototype-guided interpretable compatibility modeling scheme, PAICM, which is capable of not only determining the outfit compatibility, but also locating the discordance of incompatible outfits as well as providing the alternative item suggestion. We employ the NMF to discover the latent compatible (incompatible) attribute interaction prototypes, which are regarded as the templates to guide the discordant attribute interpretation and alternative item suggestion. Extensive experiments have been conducted on the real-world Dataset I and the promising empirical results demonstrate the effectiveness of PAICM. In addition, we found that the NMF has remarkable advantages of discovering latent factors in the context of clothing matching.

CHAPTER 6

Personalized Compatibility Modeling

6.1 INTRODUCTION

In Chapter 5, we studied how to enhance the interpretability of compatibility modeling [30] by introducing the prototype learning. However, one important factor affecting the compatibility assessment—the user factor, has been overlooked. As different people may hold different tastes in clothing matching, this chapter extends the traditional general compatibility modeling to the personalized compatibility modeling.

In a sense, most of the existing work attempts to tackle the clothing matching problem by modeling the compatibility between fashion items from the aesthetic perspective based on the visual and contextual contents of fashion items, but overlooks the role of user factor. Indeed, aesthetics can be rather subjective, as different people may have different tastes in clothing matching. For example, for the same fashion item "high-neck pullover" occurred in the first outfit of all three users in Figure 6.1, *user*1 coordinates it with the "point button tweed tight skirt," while *user*3 prefers to match it with the "check flare skirt with belt." Consequently, it is inappropriate to ignore the user context factor and access the compatibility between fashion items universally across different individuals. To bridge this gap, this work aims to tackle the personalized clothing matching problem, where without loss of generality, we focus on the compatibility modeling between the top and bottom while considering the user context.

However, the personalized compatibility modeling between fashion items is non-trivial due to the following challenges: (1) although there are many public datasets toward the general compatibility modeling and personalized fashion item recommendation tasks, respectively, there is a lack of the large-scale benchmark dataset for personalized compatibility modeling. Accordingly, how to construct a large-scale benchmark dataset to facilitate the evaluation of the proposed method constitutes a tough challenge; (2) how to seamlessly encode the user preference on clothing matching into the personalized compatibility modeling between fashion items and thus enable the matching results not only to meet the common matching patterns but also to cater to the user personal taste poses another challenge; and (3) fashion items can be comprehensively characterized by multiple modalities, such as the visual images and contextual descriptions, both of which may convey important cues on user preferences. For example, the visual signal can reveal the intuitive features user prefers, like the color and shape, while the contextual modality

Figure 6.1: Examples of users' outfit compositions.

may deliver the user preferred item brand or fabric. Therefore, how to fully take advantage of the multi-modal data in the context of the personalized clothing matching is a crucial challenge.

To address the aforementioned challenges, we present a personalized compatibility modeling scheme for clothing matching, named GP-BPR, as shown in Figure 6.2, which is able to measure the compatibility between fashion items from not only the general aesthetics but also the personal preference perspectives. In particular, GP-BPR consists of two essential components: *general compatibility modeling* and *personal preference modeling*. The content-based general compatibility modeling works on learning the latent compatibility space shared by complementary items to characterize the item-item interactions toward clothing matching. Meanwhile, the personal preference modeling focuses on exploiting the latent preference factor based on the multi-modal data of fashion items and hence captures the user-item interactions comprehensively. Ultimately, based on the BPR framework [100], GP-BPR jointly integrates the general compatibility and personal preference modeling. To facilitate the evaluation, we construct a large-scale dataset from the online fashion community IQON,[1] which comprises 308,747 outfits created by 3,568 users with 672,335 fashion items.

6.2   RELATED WORK

Owing to the recent booming of the fashion industry, increasing research attentions from both the computer vision and multimedia communities have been paid to the fashion domain, espe-

---
[1]https://www.iqon.jp/

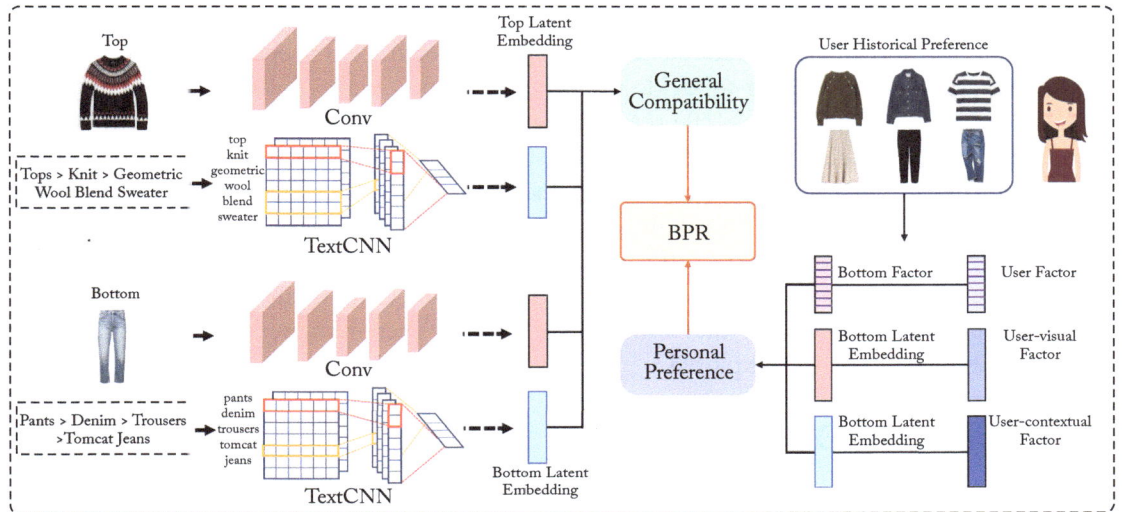

Figure 6.2: Illustration of the proposed scheme. The general compatibility modeling aims to learn the visual and contextual latent embedding of the items. The personal compatibility modeling focuses on exploiting the latent user-item interaction factors to capture the user preference. These two components are integrated by the BPR framework to jointly tackle the personalized clothing matching problem.

cially the clothing matching problem [24, 28, 31, 67, 108], which is usually cast as the compatibility modeling task between complementary fashion items. For example, Li et al. [67] proposed an outfit quality predictor with the multi-modal multi-instance deep learning based on item appearance. In addition, Song et al. [108] introduced a content-based neural scheme toward the compatibility modeling between fashion items based on their multi-modal data. Later, Yang et al. [127] presented a translation-based neural fashion compatibility modeling framework, which jointly optimizes the fashion item embeddings and category-specific complementary relations in an end-to-end manner. Moreover, noticing that the fashion domain has accumulated various valuable knowledge that can be helpful to guide the compatibility modeling, Song et al. [109] shed light on integrating the rich fashion domain knowledge to the pure data-driven learning, where a neural compatibility modeling scheme with attentive knowledge distillation was presented. Although existing efforts have achieved compelling success, they mainly focused on modeling the compatibility between fashion items purely based on the general item-item compatibility and overlooked the user factor in the compatibility modeling, which is the major concern of our work.

In addition, personalized recommendation in fashion domain also gains great research attentions [9, 36, 114]. In particular, existing personalized recommendation work in fashion domain [34, 43, 110] mainly utilized the MF framework to model user preferences based on their feedback with real-world datasets. For example, Hu et al. [43] proposed a functional tensor factorization model aiming to tackle the problem of personalized outfit recommendation based on a dataset comprising of 150 users. Although this method is effective in the whole outfit recommendation, the cold start problem constitutes a remaining issue that worths further exploring. Toward this end, He et al. [34] introduced a scalable matrix factorization model that incorporates the visual signal of items into the user preference predictors to fulfill the recommendation task. In a sense, existing efforts focus on exploring the latent user-item interactions to tackle the personalized recommendation problems. Beyond that, in this work, we aim to fulfill the task of personalized clothing matching, where both the user-item preference and item-item compatibility need to be well explored.

6.3 METHODOLOGY

In this section, we first give the research problem formulation and then detail the proposed personalized compatibility modeling scheme, GP-BPR.

6.3.1 PROBLEM FORMULATION

Suppose we have a set of users $\mathcal{U} = \{u_1, u_2, \ldots, u_M\}$, a set of tops $\mathcal{T} = \{t_1, t_2, \ldots, t_{N_t}\}$, and a set of bottoms $\mathcal{B} = \{b_1, b_2, \ldots, b_{N_b}\}$, where M, N_t, and N_b denote the total numbers of users, tops, and bottoms, respectively. Each user u_m is associated with a set of historically composed top-bottom pairs $\mathcal{O}_m = \{(t_{i_1^m}, b_{j_1^m}), (t_{i_2^m}, b_{j_2^m}), \ldots, (t_{i_{N_m}^m}, b_{j_{N_m}^m})\}$, where $i_k^m \in [1, 2, \ldots, N_t]$ and $j_k^m \in [1, 2, \ldots, N_b]$ refer to the index of the top and bottom. For each t_i (b_i), we use $\mathbf{v}_i^t$ ($\mathbf{v}_i^b$) $\in \mathbb{R}^{D_v}$ and $\mathbf{c}_i^t$ ($\mathbf{c}_i^b$) $\in \mathbb{R}^{D_c}$ to represent its visual and contextual embeddings, respectively. D_v and D_c denote the dimensions of the corresponding embeddings.

As a matter of fact, different people may have different fashion tastes and thus prefer different clothing items to make favorable outfits. Accordingly, in this work, we aim to tackle the essential compatibility modeling between fashion items for clothing matching by taking the user factor into account. Without loss of generality, we particularly investigate the problem of "which bottom would be preferred by the user to match the given top." Let p_{ij}^m denote the preference of the user u_m toward the bottom b_j for top t_i, based on which we can generate a personalized ranking list of bottoms b_j's for a given top t_i and hence solve the practical problem of personalized clothing matching. In particular, to accurately measure p_{ij}^m, we focus on devising a personalized compatibility modeling network $\mathcal{F}$, which is capable of compiling the user preference context into the compatibility modeling between fashion items as follows:

$$p_{ij}^m = \mathcal{F}\left(t_i, b_j, u_m | \Theta_F\right), \tag{6.1}$$

where Θ_F refers to the to-be-learned model parameters.

In a sense, toward personalized clothing matching (e.g., matching a bottom for a user's top), it is natural to incorporate both the item-item compatibility and the user-item preference.

In light of this, we measure the user preference toward a bottom for a given to-be-matched top based on both the general compatibility modeling and the personal preference modeling. Formally, we have

$$\begin{cases} p_{ij}^m = \mu \cdot s_{ij} + (1 - \mu) \cdot c_{mj}, \\ s_{ij} = \mathcal{G}\left(t_i, b_j | \Theta_G\right), \\ c_{mj} = \mathcal{P}\left(u_m, b_j | \Theta_P\right), \end{cases} \tag{6.2}$$

where $\mathcal{G}$ and $\mathcal{P}$ correspond to the general compatibility modeling and personal preference modeling networks, respectively. Θ_G and Θ_P are the corresponding model parameters. s_{ij} denotes the general compatibility between the top t_i and bottom b_j, while c_{mj} represents the personal preference of user u_m toward the bottom b_j. μ is the non-negative tradeoff parameter to control the relative importance of both components.

6.3.2 GENERAL COMPATIBILITY MODELING

To measure the general compatibility between fashion items, similar to [108], we aim to seek the latent space where the compatibility between complementary fashion items can be well captured by the distance between their latent representations. In particular, we adopt the MLP again, owing to its superior performance in various representation learning tasks [12, 74, 123]. To comprehensively characterize each fashion item and enhance the general compatibility modeling, we utilize both (i.e., the visual and contextual) modality signals. Here, we take the visual representation learning of tops as an example. Given the i-th top $\mathbf{v}_i^t$, we have

$$\begin{cases} \mathbf{h}_{i1}^t = s\left(\mathbf{W}_1^t \mathbf{v}_i^t + \mathbf{b}_1^t\right), \\ \mathbf{h}_{ik}^t = s\left(\mathbf{W}_k^t \mathbf{h}_{i(k-1)}^t + \mathbf{b}_k^t\right), \quad k = 2, \ldots, K, \end{cases} \tag{6.3}$$

where $\mathbf{h}_{ik}^t$ denotes the hidden representation, $\mathbf{W}_k^t$ and $\mathbf{b}_k^t, k = 1, \ldots, K$, are the weight matrices and biases, respectively. $s : \mathbb{R} \mapsto \mathbb{R}$ is the nonlinear activation function applied element wise.[2] We treat the output of the K-th layer as the latent visual embedding for the top, i.e., $\tilde{\mathbf{v}}_i^t = \mathbf{h}_{iK}^t \in \mathbb{R}^{D_{v0}}$, where D_{v0} denotes the dimensionality of the latent compatibility space.

In the similar manner, we can also derive the latent contextual embedding for the top t_i, and the visual and contextual embeddings for the bottom b_j as $\tilde{\mathbf{c}}_i^t, \tilde{\mathbf{v}}_j^b$, and $\tilde{\mathbf{c}}_j^b$, respectively. Thereafter, to comprehensively measure the general compatibility, we define,

$$s_{ij} = \pi \left(\tilde{\mathbf{v}}_i^t\right)^T \tilde{\mathbf{v}}_j^b + (1 - \pi)\left(\tilde{\mathbf{c}}_i^t\right)^T \tilde{\mathbf{c}}_j^b, \tag{6.4}$$

where π is the non-negative trade-off parameter, calibrating the relative importance of the modalities. s_{ij} denotes the general compatibility between the top t_i and bottom b_j.

---

[2]In this work, we use the sigmoid function $s(x) = 1/(1 + e^{-x})$.

6.3.3   PERSONAL PREFERENCE MODELING

As for the personal preference modeling toward a bottom, we resort to the matrix factorization framework, which has shown great success in personalized recommendation tasks [2, 56, 60, 92]. The underlying philosophy is to decompose the user-item interaction matrix into the latent user factors and item factors, whose inner products encode the user-item interaction scores. In our context, we model the user preference toward a bottom as follows:

$$c_{mj} = \alpha + \beta_m + \beta_j + \boldsymbol{\gamma}_m^T \boldsymbol{\gamma}_j, \tag{6.5}$$

where c_{mj} represents the preference of user u_m for bottom b_j. α is the to-be-learned global offset, and β_m and β_j are the user u_m and bottom b_j bias terms. $\boldsymbol{\gamma}_m$ and $\boldsymbol{\gamma}_j$ are the latent factors of user u_m and bottom b_j, respectively, whose inner product captures the latent preference of user u_m for the bottom b_j.

Apart from the latent overall preference factors, inspired by [34], we also incorporate the latent content-based preference factors. The philosophy behind lies in that the user preference for a fashion item may come from the visual characteristics, like the color and shape, or the contextual features, like the brand and material. Different from [34], we take into account of not only visual modality but also contextual modality of fashion items to comprehensively measure the user-item interactions. Accordingly, incorporating the latent visual and contextual preference factors to the matrix factorization framework, we have $c_{mj} =$

$$\alpha + \beta_m + \beta_j + \boldsymbol{\gamma}_m^T \boldsymbol{\gamma}_j + \eta \left(\boldsymbol{\xi}_m^v\right)^T \boldsymbol{\xi}_j^v + (1 - \eta) \left(\boldsymbol{\xi}_m^c\right)^T \boldsymbol{\xi}_j^c, \tag{6.6}$$

where $\boldsymbol{\xi}_m^v$ and $\boldsymbol{\xi}_j^v$ are the latent visual factors of user u_m and bottom b_j, respectively. The inner product between them conveys the visual preference interaction between the user u_m and bottom b_j. Similarly, $\boldsymbol{\xi}_m^c$ and $\boldsymbol{\xi}_j^c$ stand for the latent contextual factors of user u_m and bottom b_j, respectively, which compile the contextual preference interaction. In this work, we make $\boldsymbol{\xi}_j^v = \tilde{\mathbf{v}}_j^b$ and $\boldsymbol{\xi}_j^c = \tilde{\mathbf{c}}_j^b$, where $\tilde{\mathbf{v}}_j^b$ and $\tilde{\mathbf{c}}_j^b$ are the latent embeddings for the visual and contextual representations of bottom b_j. η is the non-negative tradeoff parameter.

6.3.4   OPTIMIZATION

To accurately model the implicit interaction among users and fashion items (i.e., tops and bottoms), we adopt the BPR framework, which has proven to be powerful in the pair-wise implicit preference modeling [6, 78, 82]. In particular, we first construct the following training set $\mathcal{D} :=$

$$\left\{ (m, i, j, k) | u_m \in \mathcal{U} \wedge (t_i, b_j) \in \mathcal{O}_m \wedge b_k \in \mathcal{B} \backslash b_j \right\}, \tag{6.7}$$

where the quadruplet (m, i, j, k) indicates that to match the given top t_i and make a proper outfit, the user u_m prefers the bottom b_j to b_k. Then according to the BPR loss [100], we thus have the following objective function:

$$\mathcal{L} = \sum_{(m,i,j,k)\in\mathcal{D}} l_{bpr}\left(p_{ij}^m, p_{ik}^m\right) + \frac{\lambda}{2}\left\|\Theta_F\right\|_F^2 ,$$

$$= \sum_{(m,i,j,k)\in\mathcal{D}} \left[-\ln\left(\sigma\left(p_{ij}^m - p_{ik}^m\right)\right)\right] + \frac{\lambda}{2}\left\|\Theta_F\right\|_F^2 , \tag{6.8}$$

where λ is the non-negative hyperparameter, the last term is designed to avoid overfitting, and Θ_F refers to the set of parameters (i.e., $\mathbf{W}_k^x$, $\mathbf{b}_k^x$, α, β_m, β_j, γ_m, γ_j, ξ_m^v and ξ_m^c) of the model. Figure 6.3 illustrates the workflow of our model, and the optimization procedure of our framework is summarized in Algorithm 6.3.

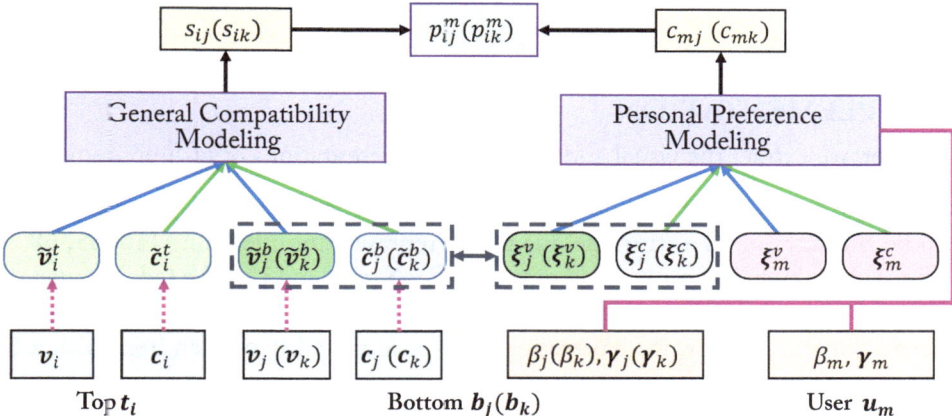

Figure 6.3: Workflow of the proposed personalized compatibility modeling framework.

6.4 EXPERIMENT

To evaluate the proposed method, we conducted extensive experiments on the real-world Dataset II by answering the following research questions.

- Does the proposed GP-BPR outperform the state-of-the-art methods?

- What is the contribution of the personal preference modeling as compared to that over the general compatibility?

- How does GP-BPR perform in the application of the personalized complementary fashion item retrieval?

In this section, we first detail the implementation and then provide the experimental results on each of the above research question.

Algorithm 6.3 Personalized Compatibility Modeling.

Input: Training set $\mathcal{D} = \{(m, i, j, k)\}$, learning rate ρ, regularization parameter λ, trade-off parameters π, η, and μ.

Output: Parameters Θ_F.

1: Initialize parameters Θ_F.
2: **repeat**
3:     Draw (m, i, j, k) from $\mathcal{D}$.
4:     Compute p_{ij}^m according to Eq. (6.2).
5:     **for** each parameter θ in Θ_F **do**
6:         Update $\theta \leftarrow \theta + \rho(\sigma(-p_{ij}^m)\frac{p_{ij}^m}{\theta} - \lambda\theta)$.
7:     **end for**
8: **until** Converge

6.4.1   IMPLEMENTATION

In this chapter, we extract the visual and contextual representations of fashion items as follows.

Visual Modality. Regarding the visual modality, we applied the deep CNNs, which has proven to be the state-of-the-art model for image representation learning [10, 55, 68, 72]. In particular, we chose the 50-layer residual network (ResNet50) in [33]. We fed the image of each fashion item to the network, and adopted the output of the last average pooling layer as the visual representation. Thereby, we represented the visual modality of each item with a 2048-D vector.

Contextual Modality. As a pioneering attempt of the personalized clothing matching, here we only considered the title description and category metadata as the contextual information of the fashion item. We first tokenized the text with the help of the Japanese morphological analyzer Kuromoji.[3] To obtain the effective contextual representation, instead of the traditional linguistic features [106, 107], we adopted the CNN architecture [57], which has achieved compelling success in various natural language processing tasks [45, 102]. In particular, we first represented each contextual description as a concatenated word vector, where each row represents one constituent word. To represent each word, we employed the 300-D vector provided by the Japanese word2vec *Nwjc2vec* in the search mode, which is created from NINJAL Web Japanese Corpus [103]. We then deployed the single-channel CNN, consisting of a convolutional layer on top of the concatenated word vectors and a max pooling layer. In particular, we used four kernels with sizes of 2, 3, 4, and 5, respectively. For each kernel, we had 100 feature maps. We employed the rectified linear unit (ReLU) as the activation function. Ultimately, we obtained a 400-D contextual representation for each item.

---

[3]http://www.atilika.org/

Experiment Settings. In our context of matching bottoms for a given top, we only considered the outfits that either contain a top and a bottom, or a coat plus a bottom/dress, where we treated the coat as the "top" while the bottom/dress as the "bottom." As one user may coordinate different shoes or accessories for the same top-bottom pair to make different outfits, we removed the duplicated top-bottom pairs from the dataset, resulting in 217,806 unique top-bottom pairs. Regarding the evaluation, we adopted the leave-one-out strategy, where we randomly sampled one top-bottom pair for each user and retained it as the testing sample. Then we generated the quadruple set $\mathcal{T}_{train}$, $\mathcal{D}_{valid}$, and $\mathcal{D}_{test}$ according to Eq. (6.7), where for each positive top-bottom pair (t_i, b_j) of the user u_m, we randomly sampled a negative bottom b_k from the whole bottom dataset (i.e., $\mathcal{B}$) to comprise a quadruplet (m, i, j, k). Finally, we adopted the AUC [133] as the evaluation metric.

For optimization, we employed the adaptive moment estimation method (Adam) [58]. We adopted the grid search strategy to determine the optimal values for the regularization parameter λ and trade-off parameters (π, η, and μ). In addition, the mini-batch size, the number of hidden units and learning rate were searched in [32, 64, 128], [256, 512, 1024], and [0.0005, 0.001, 0.005, 0.01], respectively. The proposed model was fine-tuned for 40 epochs, and the performance on the testing set was reported. We empirically set the number of hidden layers in representation learning $K = 1$.

6.4.2   ON MODEL COMPARISON (RQ1)

We chose the following state-of-the-art methods as the baselines to evaluate the proposed model.

- **POP-T**: We used the "popularity" of the bottom to measure its compatibility with top, which is defined as the number of outfits that the bottom appeared in the training set.

- **POP-U**: Similarly, in this baseline, we defined the "popularity" of the bottom as the number of users who once interacted with the bottom in the training set.

- **RAND**: We randomly assigned the compatibility scores of m_{ij} and m_{ik} between items.

- **Bi-LSTM**: We chose the bidirectional LSTM model in [31] which explores the outfit compatibility by sequentially predicting the next item conditioned on previous ones. In our context, we adapted Bi-LSTM to deal with an outfit comprising of a top and a bottom.

- **BPR-DAE**: We selected the content-based neural scheme introduced by [108] that is capable of jointly modeling the coherent relation between different modalities of fashion items and the implicit preference among items via a dual autoencoder network. It is worth noting that BPR-DAE overlooks the user factor in the compatibility modeling.

- **BPR-MF**: We used the pairwise ranking method introduced in [100], where the latent user-item relations are captured by the MF method.

- **VBPR**: We adopted the VBPR in [34], which exploits the visual data of fashion items with the factorization method to recommend an item for the user.

- **TBPR**: We derived TBPR from VBPR by replacing the visual signals with the contextual modality of fashion items.

- **VTBPR**: We extended VBPR in [34] by further introducing the context factor to comprehensively characterize the user's preference from both the visual and contextual perspectives.

Table 6.1 shows the performance comparison among different approaches. From this table, we have the following observations. (1) BPR-DAE shows superiority over Bi-LSTM, which implies that the content-based scheme performs better than the sequential model in the general compatibility modeling between fashion items. (2) VTBPR outperforms VBPR, TBPR, and BPR-MF, which confirms the advantage of considering both the visual and contextual modalities in the personal preference modeling. Interestingly, we found that TBPR slightly surpasses VBPR, demonstrating the great potential of contextual data in characterizing users' personal preference of items. (3) GP-BPR achieves better performance than all the other methods that focus on either the general compatibility modeling or person preference modeling, validating the necessity of incorporating both the general item-item compatibility and user-item preference in the context of personalized clothing matching.

Table 6.1: Performance comparison among different approaches in terms of AUC

Approach	AUC
POP-T	0.6042
POP-U	0.5951
RAND	0.5014
Bi-LSTM	0.6739
BPR-DAE	0.7096
BPR-MF	0.7958
VBPR	0.8170
TBPR	0.8190
VTBPR	0.8232
GP-BPR	**0.8388**

To evaluate the contribution of each modality in our model, we further compared GP-BPR with its two derivatives: GP-BPR-V and GP-BPR-T, where only the visual and contextual modality of fashion items were explored, respectively. Table 6.2 shows the performance comparison of our model with different modalities. We observed that our model outperforms

Table 6.2: Performance comparison among different modalities in terms of AUC

Approach	AUC
GP-BPR-V	0.8239
GP-BPR-T	0.8313
GP-BPR	**0.8388**

both GP-BPR-V and GP-BPR-T, which suggests that the visual and contextual signals do complement each other and both contribute to the personalized compatibility modeling. In addition, similar to above TBPR and VBPR, we found that GP-BPR-T achieves better performance than GP-BPR-V. This may be due to two reasons: (1) the contextual information of fashion items can summarize the key features, such as the pattern and material, of fashion items more concisely and (2) the contextual data usually convey some high-level semantic cues, like the item brand, which obviously can facilitate not only the personal preference modeling but also the general compatibility modeling, as items of the same brand are more likely to be compatible.

6.4.3   ON COMPONENT COMPARISON (RQ2)

To gain a better understanding with respect to the contribution of each component in our model, we introduced two derivatives: G-BPR and P-BPR, where we only consider the general compatibility and personal preference modeling component of our model, respectively. Figure 6.4 shows the performance of our model with different component configurations. It can be seen that our model surpasses the derivative models, confirming the importance of each component in our model. In addition, interestingly, we noticed that P-BPR achieves better performance than that of G-BPR which suggests that the personal preference is the dominant factor affecting the individual's personalized clothing matching. To gain more detailed insights, we further checked the performance of our model with different components on seven popular bottom categories. As shown in Figure 6.4, GP-BPR outperforms the G-BPR and P-BRP consistently across different bottom categories, which reconfirms the effects of both two components. In addition, it is interesting to observe that by incorporating the general compatibility modeling, GP-BPR achieves the greatest improvement over the pure personal preference modeling component P-BPR in terms of the category "Long Skirt." One plausible explanation is that long skirts are usually critical of tops to make compatible outfits. Accordingly, taking the general compatibility modeling into account can boost the performance of P-BPR significantly. On the contrary, even with the help of the general compatibility modeling, GP-BPR shows limited superiority over P-BPR regarding the category "Denim Pants." That can be attributed to the fact that denim pants can go with various tops, ranging from coats to T-shirts, which makes incorporating the general item-item compatibility less helpful.

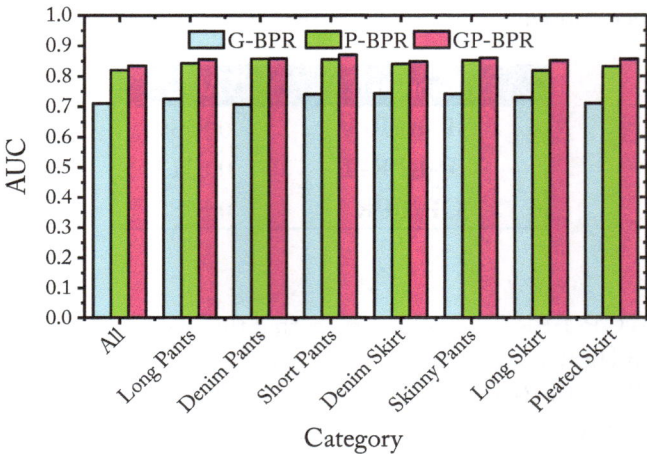

Figure 6.4: Performance of different methods on different bottom categories. "All" denotes the whole testing set.

Moreover, we also illustrate the performance of our GP-BPR with respect to the trade-off parameter μ in Figure 6.5, where μ represents the weight of the general compatibility modeling component. As we can see, when $\mu = 0.3$ and P-BPR gets a higher weight than G-BPR, our GP-BPR achieves the optimal performance, indicating the dominant effect of P-BPR to GP-BPR. In addition, we noticed that when the value of μ ranges from 0.8–1.0 and our GP-BPR degenerates into the G-BPR, there is a sharp performance decrease on GP-BPR. In a sense, this is consistent with the above observation that the general compatibility modeling component alone suffers from the poor performance in the context of personalized compatibility modeling.

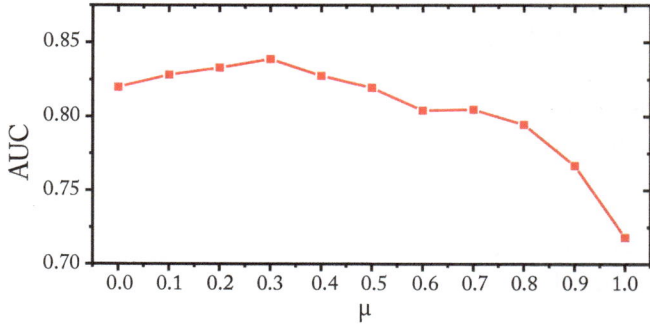

Figure 6.5: Performance of GP-BPR with respect to the trade-off parameter μ.

To intuitively show the impact of both components, we further illustrate the comparison among G-BPR, P-BPR, and GP-BPR with several testing quadruplets in Figure 6.6. Notably, as mentioned previously, each testing quadruplet (m, i, j, k) indicates that the user u_m prefers the bottom b_j than b_k to match the given top t_i. As we can see, bottoms b_j and b_k in the first example of *user*2 share the similar style with the items in the user's historical preference, making the user preference to these two bottoms hard to tell and resulting the failure of P-BPR. However, taking the general item-item compatibility into account, where the "Ocean logo T-shirt" seems to go better with the shorts rather than the long jeans, GP-BPR can get the correct evaluation result. In addition, we also found that the personal preference can boost the performance especially when the general compatibility is hard to model. As can be seen, in the second example of *user*1, the general compatibility between the top and bottom candidates should be difficult to distinguish. Fortunately, resorting to the historical preference of *user*1, our GP-BPR can also reach the right result. Overall, both the general compatibility modeling and personal preference modeling are pivotal in our model and the cooperation of these two components can boost the performance of each component.

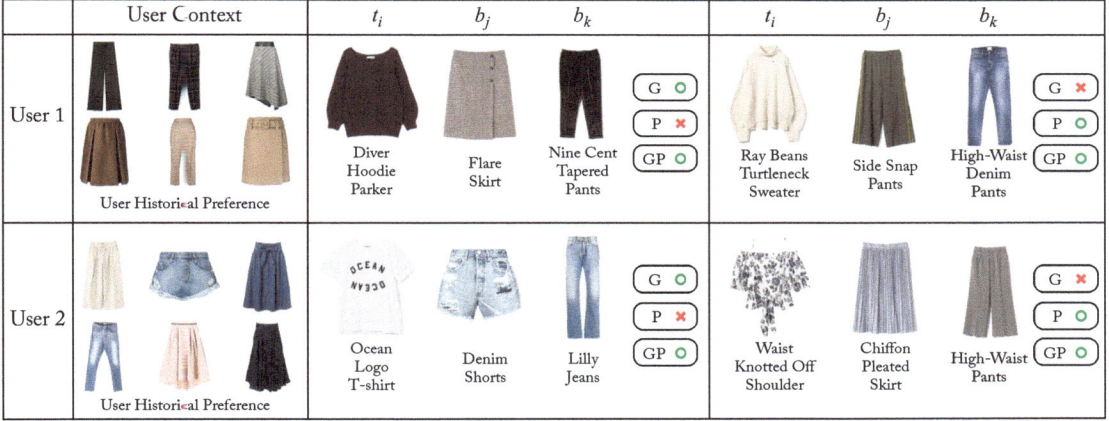

Figure 6.6: Illustration of the effect of the general compatibility and personal preference modeling. All the quadruplets satisfy the ground truth that $\{u_m, t_i\}: b_j \succ b_k$. "G "P", and "GP" are the abbreviations for G-BPR, P-BPR, and GP-BPR, respectively. We represent the correct judgments of the model with the green circle and that of the wrong with the red cross.

6.4.4   ON FASHION ITEM RETRIEVAL (RQ3)

To assess the practical value of our work, we evaluate our model toward the personalized complementary fashion item retrieval. Similar to [37], we fed each user-top pair (u_m, t_i) in $\mathcal{D}_{test}$ as the query and randomly selected T bottoms as the ranking candidates with only one positive (ground truth) bottom. Thereafter, by passing them to the trained models and calculating the compatibility score, we generated a ranking list of these bottoms for each query. In our setting, we focused on the average position of the positive bottom in the ranking list and thus adopted the MRR metric [52, 128, 129].

Figure 6.7 shows the performance of different models in terms of MRR at different numbers of the bottom candidates T. As can be seen, our GP-BPR shows superiority over all the other baselines consistently at different numbers of bottom candidates, demonstrating the effectiveness of our model in the personalized complementary fashion item retrieval. Moreover, to get a better understanding of our GP-BPR in this context, in Figure 6.8, we listed the ranking results of GP-BPR and its derivatives G-BPR and P-BPR for a given query. For the query "red knit pullover," G-BPR that simply relies on the general compatibility modeling, does rank the compatible bottoms at first places, including the positive one. Then further taking the user (historical) preference factor into account, we found that GP-BPR can boost the rank of the positive bottom from the fourth place to the first one, which verifies the importance of the user factor.

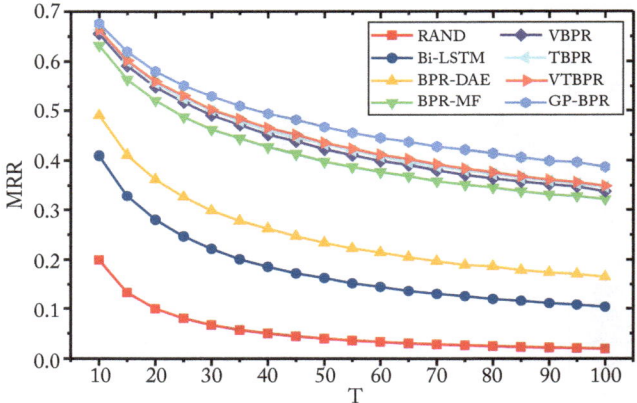

Figure 6.7: Performance of different approaches with respect to MRR at different numbers of the bottom candidates T.

6.5   SUMMARY

In this chapter, we present a personalized compatibility modeling scheme toward personalized clothing matching, termed GP-BPR, which measures the compatibility between fashion items from not only the general aesthetics but also the personal preference perspectives. In particular, motivated by the fact that both modalities (i.e., the visual and contextual modalities) of fashion items can deliver valuable information regarding personal preference, we integrate the visual and contextual data of fashion items into the personal preference modeling. Extensive experiments

Figure 6.8: Illustration of the ranking results. The bottoms highlighted in the red boxes are the positive ones.

have been conducted on the created Dataset II. The encouraging experiment results verify the effectiveness of the proposed scheme and indicate the necessity of integrating both the general item-item compatibility and personal user-item preference in the context of personalized clothing matching. One limitation of our work is that currently we fuse the two components of general compatibility modeling and personalized preference modeling linearly. In the future, we plan to devise a more advanced fusion strategy, such as the attentive fusion, to boost the performance.

CHAPTER 7

Personalized Capsule Wardrobe Creation

7.1 INTRODUCTION

In Chapter 6, we introduced the personalized compatibility modeling between fashion items, where the user preferences for items are exploited. In fact, apart from the user preference, the user figure, like body shape, also plays an important role in the compatibility modeling. Meanwhile, each outfit usually involves multiple fashion items, like the coat, top, bottom, and shoes, rather than only two pieces. Toward this end, this chapter extends the scheme presented in Chapter 6 to handle the personalized compatibility modeling for outfits in the context of personalized capsule wardrobe creation.

Capsule wardrobe (CW) is a minimum collection of garments (e.g., clothes and shoes), with diverse combinations to inspire people to pair up various compatible outfits [41]. Apparently, the capsule wardrobe plays a crucial role in people's daily life by saving time and money spent on dressing appropriately [63]. In practice, capsule wardrobes are usually created by fashion experts through manually selecting garments and evaluating the potential outfits. To relieve the burden of labor cost, recent researches in multimedia have generated reasonable CWs by *garment modeling* (i.e., analyzing the garment-garment compatibility) based on the visual appearances and textual descriptions of fashion items [31, 41].

However, the CW generated by existing approaches may be unsuitable for individual users because of their distinct demographics, preferences, body shapes, and consumption habits. For example, the appearance of an outfit could largely depend on whether it is suitable for the *user body shape* [38, 101]. Therefore, lacking the modeling of the user body shape may result in inappropriate outfits for the target user. Moreover, apart from the garment compatibility, whether an outfit is suitable also highly depends on the *user preference* [54]. As such, in addition to the traditional garment modeling, we argue the necessity of *user modeling* (i.e., analyzing the user-garment compatibility) to evaluate the potential outfits for the automatic CW creation. Furthermore, pursuing the practical value, we propose the *personalized capsule wardrobe (PCW)*—a collection of garments subject to creating both compatible and suitable outfits for the user.

Considering the existence of garments that have already been purchased by the user, to be cost-friendly, we formulate the automatic PCW creation task as: given the original wardrobe (i.e., a set of purchased garments) of a user, adding or deleting garments according to both user-garment and garment-garment compatibilities. As illustrated in Figure 7.1, one purchased

Figure 7.1: Illustration of the personalized capsule wardrobe (PCW) creation. Given the original wardrobe of a user, a PCW is created by adding (green box) and deleting (red box) some garments.

garment and four new garments are discarded and added to the original wardrobe, respectively, to make the resulted PCW not only presents the higher garment-garment compatibility but also caters to the user's preference and body shape. In fact, this task confronts three key challenges: (1) the PCW creation is a more complex combinatorial problem as compared to the conventional CW creation, where the complex user profile derived from the original wardrobe should be taken into account. Therefore, how to adaptively build the PCW for different individuals is the major challenge; (2) as both the outfit itself and the user profile (e.g., the preferences and body shapes) determine the outfit compatibility for a given user, how to accurately evaluate the compatibility of the potential outfit from both user-garment and garment-garment perspectives, poses another challenge; and (3) most existing datasets only support either the user preference modeling or user body shape modeling. Accordingly, the lack of dataset that facilitates the comprehensive user modeling constitutes a crucial challenge.

To tackle the aforementioned challenges, we propose a combinatorial optimization-based **P**ersonalized **C**apsule **W**ardrobe creation framework with **D**ual **C**ompatibility modeling, named PCW-DC. The key novelty of the proposed framework lies in the introduction of a *scoring model* that can comprehensively evaluate the compatibility of potential outfits from both user-garment and garment-garment perspectives. In particular, as illustrated in Figure 7.2, the scoring model consists of two key components: user modeling and garment modeling. As for the user modeling, we adopt the two most relevant aspects of the user profile: the user preference and body

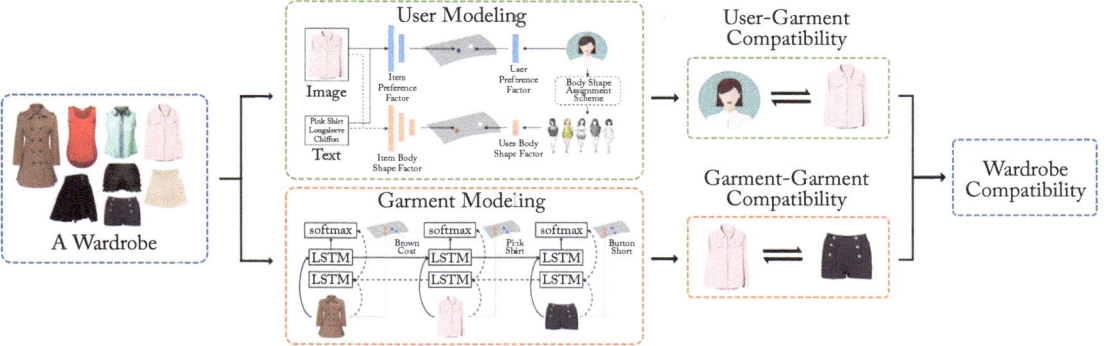

Figure 7.2: Schematic illustration of the scoring model, consisting of the user modeling and garment modeling.

shape, to measure the user-garment compatibility. To tackle the heterogeneity of user aspect and garment, we learn the user-garment compatibility in the latent matching space via a cross-modal projection. Different latent spaces are associated with different user aspects to highlight their difference for the user-garment compatibility.[1] Pertaining to the garment modeling, we adopt a bidirectional LSTM to measure the compatibility among garments, which is an efficient method to assess the outfit compatibility based on the visual appearances and textual descriptions of items. Finally, the wardrobe compatibility is estimated via the linear combination of the user modeling and garment modeling.

7.2   RELATED WORK

7.2.1   USER MODELING

User Preference Modeling. User preference modeling is gaining increasing research interest for its applications ranging from the fashion domain [34, 35] to online social networks [5, 91]. In this research line, MF has become a popular and effective framework [44, 93], which aims to uncover the latent user/item factors that affect people's preference behavior. For example, Hu et al. [44] first associated different "confidence levels" to the positive and non-observed user feedback and then perform the factorization over the user-item rating matrix. Noticing that previous works just regarded the missing feedback as negative one and failed to directly optimize the model for ranking, Rendle et al. [100] proposed a generalized BPR framework, where the user-specific order of two items is exploited by the Bayesian analysis. Thereafter, due to its great success, several extension efforts on BPR have been put forward in fashion domain. For example, He et al. [34] introduced the Visual Bayesian Personalized Ranking (VBPR), where the latent visual factor is incorporated to model the user's preference on the visual appearance of fashion

---

[1]Note that other user aspects, like age and occupation, could be easily incorporated in the similar manner.

items. Meanwhile, Yu et al. [132] presented a dynamic collaborative filtering model with the BPR optimization criterion, where the user aesthetics are exploited. Differently, in this work, we further explore the textual cues (i.e., descriptions and categories) of items to comprehensively model the user preference.

Body Shape Modeling. In a sense, body shape plays an important role in fashion analysis, as people with different body shapes tend to go with different types of items. In fact, several pioneer research efforts have been dedicated to the user body shape modeling. For example, Sattar et al. [101] first leveraged the fashion photos of users to estimate their body shapes with a multi-photo body model. Despite its great success, the loose garments in fashion photos used in this work may hide the real body shapes of users and thus make the modeling results less accurate. Meanwhile, Hidayati et al. [38] designed a clustering-based body shape assignment scheme where the body measurements of celebrities are studied. One problem this work suffers from is that the body shapes of celebrities tend to be too perfect to represent that of ordinary people, making the proposed method less practical in the real world. Beyond the existing approaches, we introduce a novel body shape assignment scheme targeting the body shape modeling for ordinary people.

7.2.2   GARMENT MODELING

Due to its pivotal role in fashion analysis, recently, several efforts have been made to study the compatibility among fashion items. For example, the authors in [87] and [116] studied the Amazon co-purchase data to model the human sense regarding the relationships between fashion items. Nevertheless, the co-purchased relation could be a weak and noisy proxy for the garment compatibility measuring, as the items purchased together can be incompatible. Accordingly, Song et al. [108] collected the outfit dataset from Polyvore and based on that introduced a content-based neural framework for the compatibility modeling between fashion items. Meanwhile, Li et al. [67] and Chen et al. [13] studied the outfit compatibility modeling that involves multiple items with the dataset collected from online fashion websites. Besides, several axillary information, such as the item category [115, 127], aesthetic characteristics [70], and domain knowledge [109, 137], has been explored to promote the performance. Recently, to enhance the practical value, there is also a growing trend to make the compatibility more interpretable, where the attention mechanism [71, 119] and interpretable feature learning [24, 83] have been explored. Noticing that existing methods mainly focus on the supervised learning and may suffer from the unreliability of the negative example sampling, several efforts [31, 41] have been made to find the latent distribution of well-matched outfits with only the positive examples. For example, Han et al. [31] regarded each outfit as an ordered sequence and utilized a bidirectional LSTM to model the outfit compatibility. Despite the great progress in garment compatibility modeling, the user factor has remained largely untapped.

7.3   PCW-DC

This section details the proposed PCW-DC. We first formulate the research problem and then detail the two key components of the scoring model: user modeling and garment modeling, based on which we can perform the PCW creation.

7.3.1   PROBLEM FORMULATION

In this work, to be cost-friendly, we focus on creating a PCW based on the user's original wardrobe (i.e., the set of historical purchased fashion items). Let $\mathcal{I}_u = \{i_{ck}^u | c = 1, \ldots, C; k = 1, \ldots, N_c\}$ be the original wardrobe of the user u, comprising a set of fashion items from C categories (e.g., the top, bottom and outer), where N_c denotes the total number of items belonging to the category c. In addition, we have a set of items $\mathcal{I} = \{i_n\}_{n=1}^N$, and each item i_n is associated with a visual image and a textual description. Our task is to generate a new personalized capsule wardrobe $\widetilde{\mathcal{I}}_u$ for the user u based on $\mathcal{I}_u$ and $\mathcal{I}$ that provides the user both compatible and suitable outfits. In a sense, we should get rid of inappropriate items from $\mathcal{I}_u$ and add proper items from $\mathcal{I}$ to maximize the user-garment and garment-garment compatibilities of the wardrobe.

Essentially, we aim to propose a comprehensive wardrobe compatibility scoring model $S(\cdot)$, based on which we can perform the PCW creation. In particular, we define $S(\cdot)$ as follows:

$$S\left(\mathcal{I}^*\right) = \alpha U\left(\mathcal{I}^* | \Theta_U\right) + (1 - \alpha)G\left(\mathcal{I}^* | \Theta_G\right), \tag{7.1}$$

where $\mathcal{I}^*$ represents a candidate wardrobe. U and G denote the compatibility modeling from the user-garment and garment-garment perspectives, respectively. α is a trade-off parameter to balance the evaluation score of each component. Θ_U and Θ_G refer to the to-be-learned model parameters of the user modeling and garment modeling, respectively.

User Preference Modeling

Intuitively, it is reasonable to argue that different individuals may prefer different item appearances and categories. For example, some people may prefer the white top instead of a black one, while others prefer the skirt rather than the short. In fact, user preference modeling in fashion domain has been studied by recent work [34], whereby two latent spaces are introduced to measure the user's overall preference and visual preference for a given item, respectively. However, this method overlooks the value of the item's textual context in the user preference modeling. In fact, the textual description, including the item title and category metadata, can summarize the key semantic features of items, like the style, material and category, and hence deliver important cues of the user preferences. Therefore, in this work, to comprehensively model the user preferences, we formulate x_{ui}^p as follows:

$$x_{ui}^p = \gamma_u^T \gamma_i + \theta_u^T \left(\mathbf{W}_p \left[f_i, t_i\right] + \beta_p\right), \tag{7.2}$$

where $\gamma_u \in \mathbb{R}^K$ and $\gamma_i \in \mathbb{R}^K$ are latent factors of the user u and the item i, respectively. $\theta_u \in \mathbb{R}^D$ is the latent content factor of the user u. $[f_i, t_i]$ refers to the concatenation of item visual feature

f_i and textual feature t_i. $\mathbf{W}_p$ and $\boldsymbol{\beta}_p$ are parameters of the nonlinear operation that maps the item features to the latent preference space. The first and second term of the equation encode the overall preference and content preference of the user u toward the item i, respectively.

For the optimization of the user preference modeling, we adopt the BPR network, which has been proven to be an effective optimization framework for the pairwise preference ranking [108]. Based on BPR, we build the following training set $\mathcal{D}_s = \{(u, i, j)\}$, where $i \in \mathcal{I}_u$ and $j \in \mathcal{I} \setminus \mathcal{I}_u$. Each triplet (u, i, j) indicates that the user u prefers the item i to the item j. Then according to [100], we have the following objective function:

$$\arg\min_{\Theta_U} \sum_{(u,i,j)\in\mathcal{D}_s} -\ln\left(\sigma\left(x_{ui}^p - x_{uj}^p\right)\right). \tag{7.3}$$

User Body Shape Modeling

As aforementioned, people with different body shapes would go with different types of items. As such, we assume that there should be a latent space where the compatibility between body shapes and item contents can be well captured. We first obtain the body shape for each user based on our body shape assignment scheme, which will be detailed in Section 4.2. Due to the fact that each user can be assigned with only one body shape, we represent each user with an one-hot encoding $\boldsymbol{u}_s \in \mathbb{R}^Q$, where Q is the total number of possible body shapes. And then, we attempt to learn the item embedding toward the body shape compatibility modeling.

On the one hand, the matching knowledge between items and body shapes can be explicitly affected by the item appearance. We thus employ the MLP to map the item content to the body shape matching space. In particular, the item embedding $\boldsymbol{i}_s \in \mathbb{R}^Q$, derived from its visual and textual features, can be designed as follows:

$$\boldsymbol{i}_s = \sigma\left(\boldsymbol{W}_s\left[\boldsymbol{f}_i, \boldsymbol{t}_i\right] + \boldsymbol{\beta}_s\right), \tag{7.4}$$

where $[\boldsymbol{f}_i, \boldsymbol{t}_i]$ is same as that in Eq. (7.2). $\boldsymbol{W}_s$ and $\boldsymbol{\beta}_s$ are the parameters of the MLP. $\sigma(x) = \frac{1}{1+\exp(-x)}$ is the nonlinear activation function.

On the other hand, the matching knowledge can be implicitly conveyed by the user's historical reviews on their purchased items, as users tend to purchase items that highlight their figure strength and hide the shortcomings. Accordingly, we define the item referenced embedding $\boldsymbol{i}_s^* \in \mathbb{R}^Q$ as follows:

$$\boldsymbol{i}_s^* = softmax\left(\sum_{u\in\mathcal{U}_i} \boldsymbol{u}_s\right), \tag{7.5}$$

where $\mathcal{U}_i$ denotes the set of users who bought the item i. $softmax(x) = \frac{\exp(x_i)}{\sum_{k=1}^{K}\exp(x_k)}$ is a normalized exponential function. Ultimately, we argue that the matching knowledge obtained from item contents and the historical reviews should be consistent, that is, the item embedding $\boldsymbol{i}_s$ and item referenced embedding $\boldsymbol{i}_s^*$ should be close. Consequently, we reach the following objective

Algorithm 7.4 Personalized Capsule Wardrobe Creation Algorithm.

Input: User original wardrobe $\mathcal{I}_u = \{i_{ck}^u\}$;
  Max and min number of item in categories $N_{\max}$ and $N_{\min}$.

1: Initialize $\mathcal{I}^0 \leftarrow \mathcal{I}_u$; $break = 0$.
2: **repeat**
3: **if** $\exists N_c \notin [N_{\min}, N_{\max}]$ **then**
4:   **if** $N_c > N_{\max}$ **then**
5:    $del = \arg\max_{i_{ck}\in\mathcal{I}^{i-1}} S(\mathcal{I}^{i-1} \setminus i_{ck})$
6:    $\mathcal{I}^i \leftarrow \mathcal{I}^{i-1}\setminus del$
7:   **else**
8:    $add = \arg\max_{i_c\in\mathcal{I}} S(\mathcal{I}^{i-1} \cup i_c)$
9:    $\mathcal{I}^i \leftarrow \mathcal{I}^{i-1}\cup add$
10:   **end if**
11: **else if** $\exists i \in \mathcal{I}^{i-1}$ s.t. $S(\mathcal{I}^{i-1} \setminus i) - S(\mathcal{I}^{i-1}) > 0$ **then**
12:   $\mathcal{I}^i \leftarrow \mathcal{I}^{i-1} \setminus i$
13: **else**
14:   $break = 1$
15: **end if**
16: **until** $break == 1$
Output: User personalized capsule wardrobe $\widetilde{\mathcal{I}}_u$.

---

function for the body shape modeling,

$$\arg\min_{\mathbf{\Theta}_U} ||\boldsymbol{i}_s^* - \boldsymbol{i}_s||^2, \tag{7.6}$$

where $||\cdot||^2$ is the Euclidean distance. Based on the well-trained model, the body shape compatibility x_{ui}^s between the item i and the user u can be calculated as follows:

$$x_{ui}^s = \boldsymbol{u}_s^T \boldsymbol{i}_s. \tag{7.7}$$

7.3.2 GARMENT MODELING

The garment-garment compatibility is another key factor affecting the PCW creation. To facilitate users to compose proper outfits, it is natural to expect that the complementary fashion items (e.g., the top, bottom and outer) in a PCW should share high compatibility and go well with each other. Toward this end, we define the garment-garment compatibility of one wardrobe $G(\mathcal{I}^*)$ as the average compatibility of the set of all potential outfits[2] $\mathcal{O}^*$ that can be generated

---

[2]Here we only consider the following three mainstream outfit patterns: top plus bottom, top plus bottom plus outer, and one-piece plus outer.

from the wardrobe $\mathcal{I}^*$. Formally, we have

$$G\left(\mathcal{I}^*|\mathbf{\Theta}_G\right) = \frac{1}{|\mathcal{O}^*|} \sum_{o_i \in \mathcal{O}^*} cmp(o_i), \tag{7.8}$$

where o_i is the i-th outfit, and $cmp(\cdot)$ refers to the outfit compatibility. To measure $cmp(o_i)$, we adopt the compatibility indicator in [31], where each outfit is treated as a sequence of items and each item is regarded as a time step input of a bidirectional LSTM. In particular, $cmp(o_i)$ can be computed as follows:

$$\begin{cases} cmp(o_i) = E_f\left(o_i; \theta_f\right) + E_b\left(o_i; \theta_b\right), \\ E_f\left(o_i; \theta_f\right) = -\frac{1}{N}\sum_{t=1}^{N} \log \Pr\left(o_{i,t+1}|o_{i,1}, \ldots, o_{i,t}; \theta_f\right), \\ E_b\left(o_i; \theta_b\right) = -\frac{1}{N}\sum_{t=N-1}^{0} \log \Pr\left(o_{i,t}|o_{i,N}, \ldots, o_{i,t+1}; \theta_b\right), \end{cases} \tag{7.9}$$

where $\Pr(\cdot|\cdot)$ stands for the conditional probability. $E_f(o_i; \theta_f)$ and $E_b(o_i; \theta_b)$ refer to the forward and backward probability that the outfit o_i would be a compatible one.

7.3.3   PCW CREATION

Based on the user modeling and garment modeling that enable us to comprehensively measure the overall compatibility of a given wardrobe, we can now proceed to present our framework for the automatic PCW creation. In particular, we cast the PCW creation as a combinatorial optimization problem and propose a heuristic PCW creation method, which is summarized in Algorithm 7.4. The underlying philosophy is to delete items from the original wardrobe that can degrade the overall wardrobe compatibility and add candidate items that can improve the compatibility.

Considering the practical situation, we first set the maximum and minimum numbers of items for each category in a wardrobe. For simplicity, here we uniformly set that as $N_{\max}$ and $N_{\min}$ for all categories. At each iteration, we first check whether the number of items of each category (i.e., N_c) in a wardrobe has reached the pre-assigned maximum and minimum number (i.e., $N_{\max}$ and $N_{\min}$). If $N_c < N_{\min}$ ($N_c > N_{\max}$), the algorithm would add (delete) one item of the category c that maximizes (maximally hurts) the overall wardrobe compatibility according to our wardrobe compatibility scoring model $S(\cdot)$. Otherwise, if $N_{\min} \le N_c \le N_{\max}$, the algorithm would check if there is an existing (unsuitable or redundant) item deteriorating the compatibility and removing which would boost the wardrobe compatibility. If yes, the item will be deleted. In light of this, this operation will adaptively adjust the number of items of each category, making the final PCW meeting the user's preferences over different item categories.

7.4   BODY SHAPE ASSIGNMENT SCHEME

Different from previous studies that represent user body shapes with complex body features, we resort to the three most essential body measurements[3]: bust girth, waist girth, and hip girth. These measurements can be easily derived from the average garment size of one's purchase history. Specifically, due to the different nature of these three body measurements, we adopt the size of tops to capture the bust girth of the user, and that of bottoms to determine one's waist girth and hip girth. Table 7.1 exhibits the correspondence between the women garment sizes and body measurements provided by Amazon. Moreover, we adopt the hip-bust and bust-waist differences as the key indicators to distinguish body shapes. The underlying philosophy is that the hip-bust difference can directly reflect the relationship between one's upper and lower bodies, while the bust-waist difference can intuitively capture one's waist characteristic.

Table 7.1: Women garment sizes and their corresponding body measurements (in inch) provided by Amazon

Size	Bust	Waist	Hip
S	34	26	36.5
M	36	28	38.5
L	38.5	30.5	41

To guide the body shape assignment, we first seek the standard hip-bust and bust-waist differences as the reference. As listed in Table 7.1, the hip-bust and bust-waist differences are invariant across different garment sizes, which thus propels us to set the standard hip-bust and bust-waist differences as 2.5 in. and 8 in., respectively. By comparing with the standard reference, we define five common body shapes with their intuitive appearances: (1) pear shape; (2) hourglass shape; (3) rectangle shape; (4) apple shape; and (5) strawberry shape. The detailed derivation rules are illustrated in Figure 7.3. Here we take the pear shape as an example, while the others can be derived in the similar manner. We define that if the user's hip-bust difference is larger than the standard one with at least 2 in. (i.e., with a plump lower body), then the user's body shape belongs to the pear shape.

7.5   EXPERIMENTS

To evaluate the proposed method, we conducted extensive experiments on bodyFashion by answering the following questions.

- Does the PCW-DC outperform the state-of-the-art baselines?

- How do the user modeling and garment modeling affect the PCW creation?

[3]https://www.iso.org/standard/65246.html/

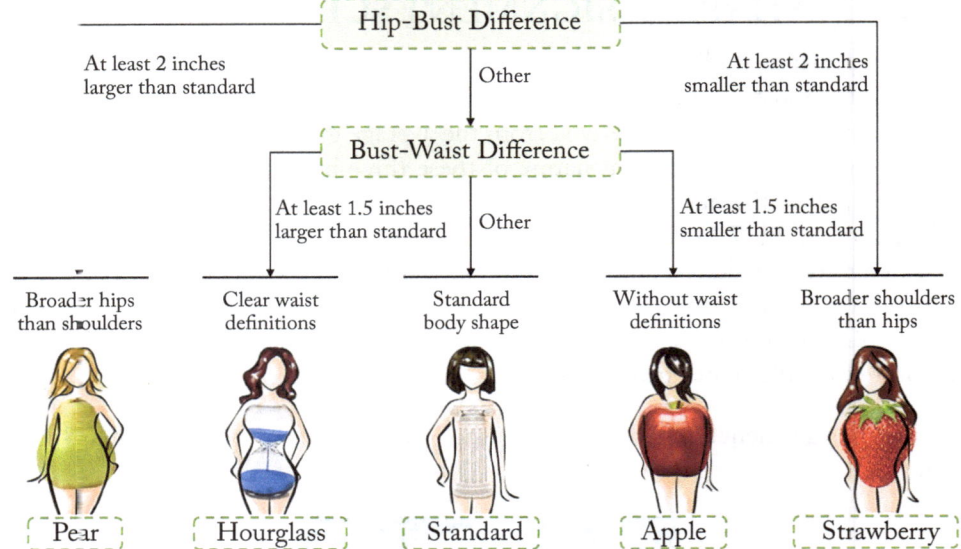

Figure 7.3: Body shape assignment scheme.

• Does the body shape modeling help people with suitable dress?

7.5.1   EXPERIMENT SETTINGS

Here, we will introduce the visual and textual representation extraction for fashion items, and the parameter settings for experiments.

Visual Representation. Convolutional networks have shown great success in various computer vision tasks, ranging from the image classification [136] to the item retrieval [53]. In particular, we chose the pre-trained ConvNet provided by [105], which consists of 16 convolutional layers followed by 3 fully connected layers. Accordingly, we fed each fashion item image to the ConvNet, and obtained a 4,096-D vector as the visual representation.

Textual Representation. To extract meaningful cues from the textual description, we focused on the descriptive words toward the attribute characterization of the item. Taking the 1,000 descriptive attributes defined in Deepfashion [80] as the reference, we obtained 393 descriptive words from our bodyFashion dataset. Considering the lack of color attribute, we complemented the vocabulary with extra 127 color-related descriptive words, leading to the final vocabulary consisting of 520 words. Regarding the category metadata, we re-summarized nine categories from the raw data: *outer*, *short tops*, *long tops*, *short bottoms*, *long bottoms*, *skirts*, *suits*, *dresses*, and *shoes*, where extremely fine-grained categories, like pants and leggings, are merged. Ultimately, based on the bag-of-word scheme, we represented the textural modality of each item as a 529-D vector.

Parameter Setting. To control the total number of items in the wardrobe, the maximum and minimum numbers of items in each category (i.e., N_{max} and N_{min}) are set to 5 and 3, respectively. We adopted the grid search strategy to determine the optimal value for the regularization parameter (i.e., α) in the range of [0, 1] with a step of 0.1. The numbers of hidden units for the user preference modeling, user body shape modeling and garment modeling are set as 224 (i.e., $K = 64$ and $D = 160$ in Eq. (7.2)), 512 (i.e., 256 for both visual and textual representation), and 512, respectively. As aforementioned, the garment modeling is trained on the dataset in [31], while the user modeling is learned by our bodyFashion. We then randomly sampled 180 users from bodyFashion as the testing set, on which the model performance is reported.

7.5.2   ON MODEL COMPARISON (RQ1)

To evaluate the proposed PCW creation scheme, we chose the following baselines.

- **POP.** We added/deleted items according to its "popularity," which is defined as the number of users that have purchased the item.

- **RAND.** We randomly added/deleted items to create PCWs.

- **Item Similarity Based Method (ISBM).** We added/deleted an item according to its average visual similarity to each item in the user original wardrobe, measured by the inner product of their visual features extracted by ConvNet.

- **Capsule Wardrobe Creation (CWC).** Focusing on the outfit compatibility and versatility, this method [41] creates the capsule wardrobes using a topic model over the item attributes. Here, we directly adopted the descriptive words as the item attributes.

- **Dynamic Collaborative Filtering (DCF-A).** This user preference modeling approach [132] incorporates the aesthetic features to boost the performance for item recommendation. We adapted it as one baseline by dropping the time factor that is unavailable in our context and adopting the state-of-the-art aesthetic features [112].

- **ExDCF-A.** We extended DCF-A by introducing our garment modeling score to its final recommendation score of each garment for a user, where the linear fusion with equal weights is adopted.

As it is intractable to obtain the exact ground-truth, we introduced the following three metrics to softly evaluate the PCW creation: successful rate (SR), average improvement (AI), and average diminishment (AD), whose definitions are given as follows:

$$\begin{cases} SR = \frac{|\mathcal{A}|}{|\Omega|}, \\ AI = \frac{1}{|\Omega|} \sum_{\widetilde{\mathcal{I}}_u \in \mathcal{A}} S\left(\widetilde{\mathcal{I}}_u\right) - S\left(\mathcal{I}_u\right), \\ AD = \frac{1}{|\Omega|} \sum_{\widetilde{\mathcal{I}}_u \in \Omega \setminus \mathcal{A}} S\left(\widetilde{\mathcal{I}}_u\right) - S\left(\mathcal{I}_u\right), \end{cases} \qquad (7.10)$$

where Ω is the set of testing users. $\mathcal{A} = \{\widetilde{\mathcal{I}}_u \mid S(\widetilde{\mathcal{I}}_u) - S(\mathcal{I}_u) > 0\} \subseteq \Omega$ is the set of successfully created PCWs, which are defined as those whose compatibilities, assessed by our scoring model, get improved as compared to the original ones.

Table 7.2 shows the PCW creation results of different methods. As can be seen, PCW-DC achieves the best performance with respect to all metrics, demonstrating the superiority of the proposed PCW-DC for PCW creation. In addition, methods that overlook both the garments and user profiles (i.e., POP and RAND) perform worst, while the method that considers the naive garment interaction (i.e., ISBM) promotes the performance slightly. Comparing with the above methods, DCF-A and CWC with more advanced compatibility modeling achieve the better performance. However, due to the limited modeling perspective of each method, DCF-A and CWC still suffer from the inferior performance than PCW-DC. Moreover, ExDCF-A outperforms DCF-A, which demonstrates the necessity of incorporating the user modeling to fulfill the PCW creation. To gain a better understanding, a successful example created by PCW-DC is shown in Figure 7.4. As can be seen, the somewhat monotonous original wardrobe has turned to be a versatile wardrobe by adding garments that share the similar style with the original wardrobe and deleting those hurt the overall wardrobe compatibility. Moreover, we found that most of the potential outfits of the final PCW are compatible, which meets the initial motivation of our PCW creation.

Table 7.2: Performance comparison among different methods

	SR	AI	AD
POP	8.89%	0.17%	-3.87%
RAND	11.67%	0.25%	-4.05%
ISBM	17.22%	0.32%	-3.18%
CWC [43]	20.00%	0.40%	-3.13%
DCF-A [138]	21.67%	0.48%	-2.52%
ExDCF-A	44.44%	1.10%	-1.27%
PCW-DC	68.89%	2.80%	-0.30%

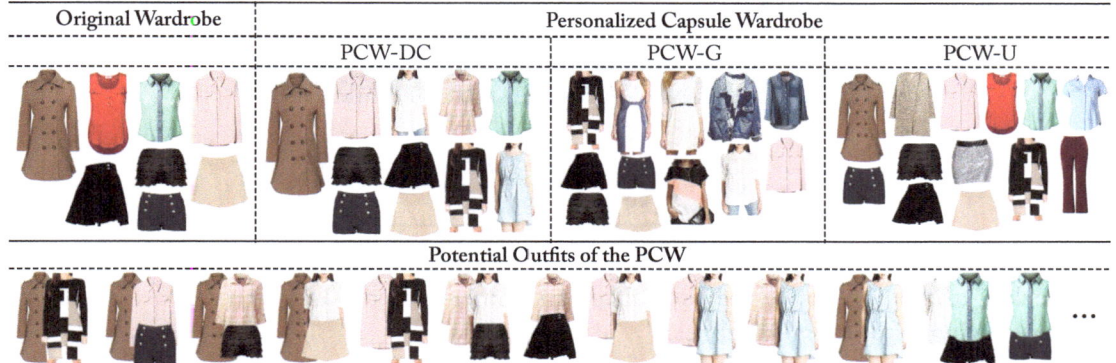

Figure 7.4: An example of PCW creation. First line: PCWs created from user original wardrobe by the proposed PCW-DC method and its variants. Second line: Possible outfits provided by the created personalized capsule wardrobe.

7.5.3   ON ABLATION STUDY (RQ2)

To verify the necessity of both the user modeling and garment modeling in the PCW creation, we further conducted the ablation study. In particular, we compared our framework with its two derivatives: the PCW creation taking the user modeling only (PCW-U) and that admitting the garment modeling only (PCW-G). It is worth noting that PCW-U and PCW-G can be effortlessly derived by setting $\alpha = 1$ and $\alpha = 0$ in Eq. (7.1), respectively.

Table 7.3 illustrates the performance of the ablation study. As can be seen, PCW-DC consistently achieves the best performance over different metrics, which verifies the importance of both the user modeling and garment modeling for the personalized wardrobe creation. In addition, PCW-G outperforms PCW-U, suggesting that the garment modeling contributes more toward the overall wardrobe compatibility modeling. One possible explanation is that the garment compatibility is the main factor during the dressing as compared to the personalized factors. To gain the deep insight, we further checked the wardrobe creation results and illustrated one example in Figure 7.4. As we can see, PCW-G retains limited garments of the original wardrobe but incorporates many external garments in different styles from the original ones. On the contrary, PCW-U follows the user's personal taste and admits garments in similar styles, but leads to several incompatible garment pairs. Beyond that, the PCW created by PCW-DC seems to be more reasonable as it not only meets the personal preferences of the user but also maintains the high garment-garment compatibility for the wardrobe.

7.5.4   ON USER BODY SHAPE MODELING (RQ3)

Here we attempted to examine the performance of the user **B**ody **S**hape **M**odeling (BSM) in our framework, which is also a major contribution of this work. In particular, we first focused

Table 7.3: Performance of different methods

	SR	AI	AD
PCW-U	42.78%	1.03%	-1.40%
PCW-G	28.89%	0.78%	-3.0%
PCW-DC	**68.89%**	**2.80%**	**-0.30%**

on checking the rationality of the body shape assignment scheme and then assessed our body shape modeling with several baselines.

Body Shape Assignment Scheme

To evaluate the body shape assignment scheme, we compared it with the method in [38], which learns the body shapes by clustering celebrities' body measurements. To adapt it for our context, we extracted the following features for each user in our dataset, including the (1) bust girth; (2) waist girth; (3) hip girth; (4) ratio between the bust and hip girths; (5) ratio between the waist and hip girths; (6) ratio between the bust and waist girths; (7) difference between the bust and hip girths; (8) difference between the waist and hip girths; and (9) difference between the bust and waist girths. According to [38], we conducted the affinity propagation clustering [25] and finally obtained six clusters. We visualized the body shape assignment results of both methods with the help of t-SNE [85] in Figure 7.5. For clear illustration, we drew two user bodies based on their body measurements with bodybuilder.[4] As can be seen, the method in [38] clusters most users into a single body shape, while checking the ground truth we found that body shapes of user1 and user2 are totally distinct. This may be attributed to the dense distribution of the body measurements of ordinary people, making it inappropriate to distinguish different body shapes with the clustering method. Meanwhile, the better performance achieved by our scheme suggests that it is advisable to explicitly model the user body shape with their body measurements.

BSM Assessment

The user body shape modeling in our PCW-DC is designed to predict the compatibility of the garment for a given body shape. To assess the effectiveness of our BSM, we adopted the accuracy of body shape prediction as the evaluation metric, where the predicted most suitable body shape and the ground truth body shape for a given garment are compared. Due to the limited related work, we chose the following baselines.

- **Probability Model (PM).** Following the work in [38], we employed the class-conditional-probability density [18] to model the global body shape matching knowledge.

---

[4]http://www.bodyvisualizer.com/

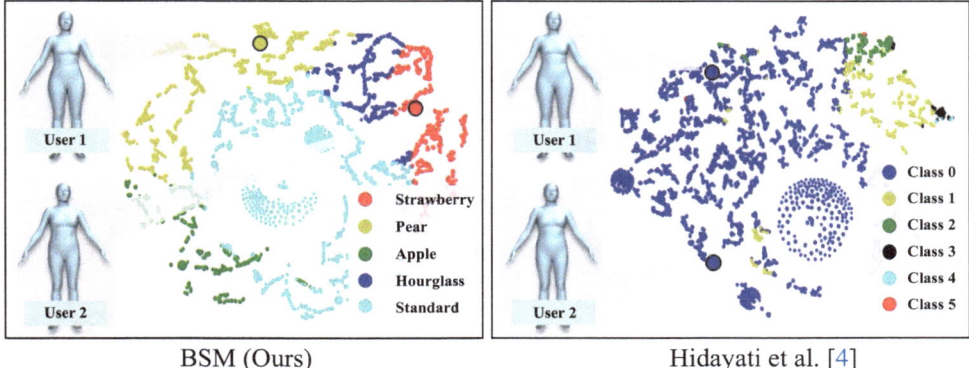

Figure 7.5: Visualization of body shape classification results.

- **BSM-V.** This method is derived from our BSM model, which takes only the garment visual appearance into account to learn the garment compatibility for the body shape.

- **BSM-T.** Similar to BSM-V, we derived this method by utilizing only the garment textural descriptions.

Table 7.4 summarizes the performance of different approaches with different category configurations. From this table, we have the following observations. (1) Our method outperforms PM, verifying the advantages of introducing the latent matching space learning with neural networks for the body shape modeling compared to the probability model. (2) BSM-V performs better than BSM-T. This may be due to the fact that the visual appearance conveys more accurate cues regarding the body shape compatibility than the textural description. (3) Our model achieves better performance than both BSM-V and BSM-T. This suggests that although textural information may deliver less significant cues than visual images for the body shape prediction, it can still boost the performance with descriptive words, like "high-waist" and "tight."

Table 7.4: Performance of different approaches in the user body shape modeling

	Outer	Top	Bottom	Suit	Total
PM [40]	0.50	0.38	0.45	0.40	0.43
BSM-V	0.48	0.45	0.45	0.61	0.50
BSM-T	0.33	0.34	0.40	0.53	0.40
BSM	0.49	**0.46**	**0.48**	**0.63**	**0.52**

Figure 7.6: Suitable and unsuitable garments for different body shapes.

To obtain more deep insights, we further investigated the most suitable and unsuitable garments for each body shape. Without loss of generality, we only considered the dresses for illustration. In particular, we fed dresses to the BSM network and obtained their latent embeddings, based on which we can derive their compatibilities for each body shape. Figure 7.6 shows three suitable and unsuitable dresses for different body shapes. It can be seen that both suitable and unsuitable garments for each body shape share certain latent garment features. For example, people in the strawberry shape are more suitable to dresses with a broad or deep neckline, while those in the pear shape would be better to wear dresses with umbrella-shaped hemlines instead of the tight ones. These observations do give plausible suggestions to help people dress properly.

7.6   SUMMARY

In this work, we study the problem of the PCW creation based on the user's original wardrobe. In particular, we present a combinatorial optimization-based personalized capsule wardrobe creation framework, named PCW-DC, with dual compatibility modeling: the user modeling and garment modeling, where the user modeling explores the user preference and user body shape. Extensive experiments have been conducted over the bodyFashion dataset, and the results demonstrate the necessity of considering both the user-garment and garment-garment compatibilities in PCW creation. Interestingly, we found that the garment-garment compatibility plays the more important role in PCW creation than the user-garment compatibility. Currently, the user modeling and garment modeling in our model are learned separately. In the future, we plan to devise an end-to-end unified scheme to boost the model performance.

CHAPTER 8

Research Frontiers

Thus far, in this book we have provided an in-depth introduction to compatibility modeling problems, ranging from the data-driven compatibility modeling to the personalized capsule wardrobe creation. To tackle these problems, we propose several general schemes for different contexts. In particular, we first introduce the great demand for automatic clothing matching scheme and identify the essential problem of compatibility modeling between fashion items. Then we analyze the prominent research challenges toward this end, such as the absence of comprehensive benchmark, comprehensive modeling, knowledge incorporation, interpretability, and subjective aesthetics. To address these issues, we present a series of compatibility modeling methods, comprising the data-driven compatibility learning, knowledge-guided compatibility modeling, prototype-wise interpretable compatibility modeling, personalized compatibility modeling, and personalized capsule wardrobe creation framework. To evaluate these theoretical methods, we create three real-world datasets collected from the online fashion communities, Polyvore, Ssense, and IQON, respectively. We have released all the involved datasets, and codes to the public[1] as illustrated in Figure 8.1.

In a sense, the theories on compatibility modeling presented in this book can benefit plenty of stakeholders of fashion industry, such as the retailers, stylists, and end-users. For retailers, especially the online ones, they usually employ professional fashion models wearing the fashion items to promote the sales. With the help of compatibility modeling, retailers can learn how to compose more eye-catching outfits and let models display for attracting the consumers to purchase. In addition, knowing which fashion items are compatible, retailers can recommend the related compatible complementary items for an item, like recommending a ripped light jeans for a T-shirt, which is more likely to raise deals when people are browsing aimlessly. Regarding the stylists, compatibility modeling can help them learn the popular compatible prototypes (i.e., attribute interactions) with the huge amount of real-word user generated data and then design suitable outfits for ordinary people. Toward end-users—the main beneficiaries, they can learn how to dress properly with the proposed automatic compatibility modeling technique without consulting stylists at great expense, and make their wardrobes concise and compact, which also undoubtedly saves both time and money expenses for end-users.

Although the above studies have shed some light on fashion compatibility modeling, we have to admit that this research line is still at young and up-and-coming stage. Here we list a few promising future research directions with their corresponding challenges.

---

[1] https://ilearnfashion.wixsite.com/compatibility-model/

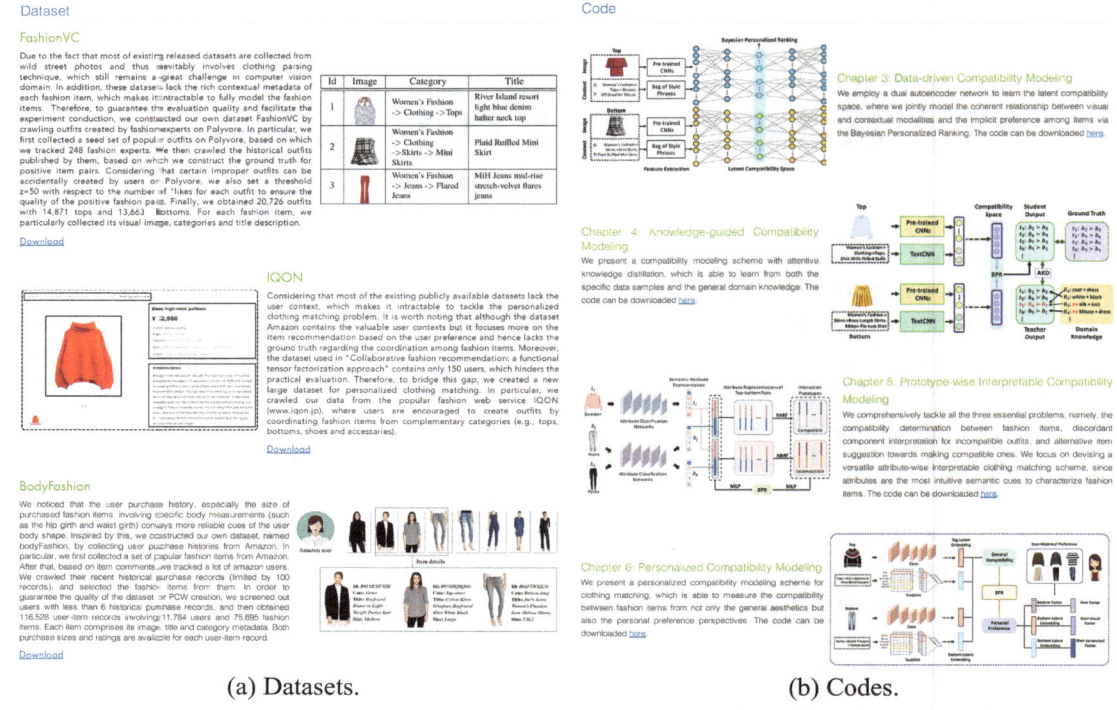

(a) Datasets.   (b) Codes.

Figure 8.1: Illustration of the website pages.

8.1   GENERATIVE COMPATIBILITY MODELING

Currently, the generative adversarial networks (GAN) have achieved great success in image generation tasks, such as image retrieval, video generation, and image synthesis, which propels the attempt of generative compatibility modeling. In the context of recommending a bottom for the given top to make a compatible outfit, if we can first generate a bottom template as an auxiliary link to the top, then the compatibility can be further modeled between the template and the given fashion item, which may improve the recommendation effect with the item-template compatibility modeling.

In light of this, the generative compatibility modeling aims to measure the compatibility between fashion items with the auxiliary complementary template generation. To the best of our knowledge, limited research studies have been devoted to the generative compatibility modeling, possibly due to the following challenges: (1) to accurately measure the compatible preference between fashion items, the latent representations are adopted for the item-item compatibility modeling. Furthermore, the compatible template for the given fashion item may contribute to the auxiliary item-template compatibility. Thus, the main challenge lies in how to seamlessly integrate the auxiliary template generation into the primary item-item compatibility modeling and boost the performance; (2) how to accurately generate a compatible bottom template for the given top to guide the item-template compatibility modeling arises the second challenge; and (3) as each fashion item may involve multiple modalities (i.e., visual and contextual modalities), both of which can convey important information toward the compatibility modeling, how to effectively fuse the multi-modal factors poses the last challenge.

In the future, we plan to enhance the compatibility measurement between fashion items by incorporating the auxiliary item-template link apart from the primary item-item correlation. On the one hand, the multi-modality information of fashion items will be considered into the item-item compatibility modeling network to comprehensively measure the compatibility between different fashion items. On the other hand, an auxiliary complementary template generation network is expected to transfer the given top to a compatible bottom template.

8.2   VIRTUAL TRY-ON WITH ARBITRARY POSE

As aforementioned that all the clothing items are served for people and the user factor, like the user body shape, plays an pivotal role in the personalized fashion compatibility modeling, the try-on effect is a major concern for people. Toward this end, owing to the recent advances in computer graphics, several efforts have been made to tackle the online virtual fitting problem with 3D modeling, such as TriMirror.[2] Despite that 3D-based methods are able to make the realistic clothing try-on, the huge labor costs for 3D annotated data and expensive scanner equipment limit their real-world applications.

Fortunately, to demonstrate fashion products more intuitively, e-commerce websites, such as Zalando,[3] usually display images of fashion models wearing their products apart from the pure product images. The tremendous publicly available images open the door to the virtual try-on with economical 2D modeling. Although several pioneer researches have achieved promising performance in the virtual try-on, existing efforts can only generate single-view results, that is, keeping the personal posture unchanged while changing the clothing item on the person. However, in reality, people may prefer to have different views wearing the outfit and then assess the compatibility. In light of this, we define a new virtual try-on task, where given a person image with the old clothing item, a personal desired pose, and a target clothing item, we aim to automatically generate a person image with the target clothing item in his/her desired pose, as illustrated in Figure 8.2.

Indeed, advanced image generation and synthesis models such as Generative Adversarial Networks (GANs) and Variational Autoencoders (VAEs) have demonstrated remarkable performance over various image generation tasks. However, it is suboptimal to directly apply these methods to solving the complex try-on task due to the following reasons. (1) In the context of virtual try-on, the body shape and desired pose of the target person highly affect the final look of

[2]https://www.trimirror.com/
[3]https://zalando.com/

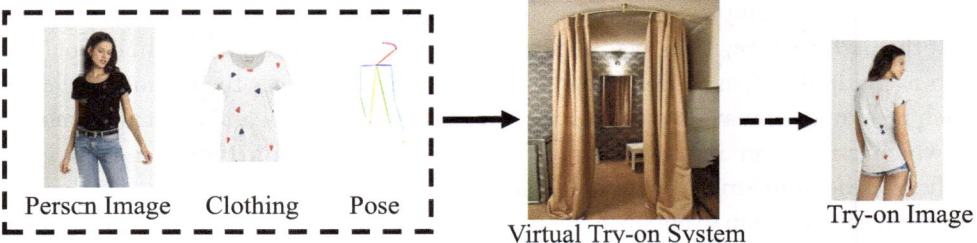

Figure 8.2: The complex try-on task.

the target clothing item on the person. Accordingly, how to properly deform the new clothing item to seamlessly align with the target person is a major challenge. (2) How to generate the try-on image that is able to maintain not only the detailed visual feature of clothing items, like texture and color, but also other parts of the person is another tough challenge. And (3) there is no large-scale benchmark dataset can support the research of complex virtual try-on. Therefore, how to create a large-scale dataset constitutes a crucial challenge.

In the future, we plan to tackle this task from the following three directions. First, we plan to predict the target body shape mask based on the conditional person image and the target pose to provide the intermediate guidance for the clothing deformation, and deform the desired clothing item aligned with the predicted body shape mask and the target pose. Second, we will focus on synthesizing the realistic try-on images by incorporating the attentive clothing-person alignment and bidirectional generation consistency into the generative adversarial networks. Last, we expect to construct a new large-scale dataset from fashion-oriented e-commercial websites which contain clothing items with their corresponding model images in different poses.

8.3   CLOTHING GENERATION

As a matter of fact, existing methods in the fashion compatibility modeling domain mainly work on datasets composed of pure clean clothing images. However, in real-world applications, compatible clothing items are more likely to be presented with people (i.e., the models), as fashion lovers are keen on posting their photographs with chic clothes in various shooting angles or scenarios. One promising way to make full use of these realistic data is to devise a scheme that is able to generate the clothing image with the best view and clean background from the fashion model photos. As a byproduct, this would also undoubtedly facilitate the application of cross-domain street-to-shop clothing retrieval.

As shown in Figure 8.3, this problem of generating clothing images from the fashion model photos can be cast as an image-to-image translation task, which is gaining increasing attention from researchers. The underlying philosophy is to fulfill the domain transfer, where

Source   Target
Domain   Domain

Figure 8.3: The transfer from *fashion model* to *clothing*, which requires transformation at both the texture and shape levels.

given an image in one domain (e.g., the fashion model image), the goal is to learn the latent mapping and generate the target image (e.g., the clothing) belonging to another domain. Although conditional generative adversarial networks (cGANs) have achieved great success in this research line [16, 88, 96], ranging from image colorization [47] to style transfer [138], their potential in clothing generation from fashion model images remains largely untapped.

Nevertheless, generating the exact clothes from the fashion model is challenging due to the following reasons: (1) although Generative Adversarial Networks (GANs) have been dominantly adopted in the field of image generation, they may suffer from the poor convergence when dealing with our task, as generating clothes from fashion model images requires the transformation at both the shape and texture levels; (2) as a prominent feature of clothing, shape plays an important role in clothing generation. Accordingly, how to seamlessly integrate the shape constraint into the generative framework poses another crucial challenge; and (3) there are certain noises such as the complex background of the fashion model image and the model's skin, which may hurt the quality of the generated clothing images.

In the future, inspired by painting, where the painter usually firstly sketches the outline and then accordingly colors it to accomplish the final painting, we plan to devise a two-stage shape-constrained clothing generative framework, comprising two key components: *shape predictor* and *texture renderer*. In particular, the shape predictor is devised to predict the intermediate shape map for the to-be-generated clothing item based on the representation learning. Then taking the predicted shape map as the constraint, the texture renderer can work on enforcing the generated clothing image to be not only realistic but also semantically correlated to the fashion model image.

Bibliography

[1] Dzmitry Bahdanau, Kyunghyun Cho, and Yoshua Bengio. Neural machine translation by jointly learning to align and translate. *CoRR*, abs/1409.0473, 2014. 33

[2] Jesús Bobadilla, Rodolfo Bojorque, Antonio Hernando Esteban, and Remigio Hurtado. Recommender systems clustering using Bayesian non-negative matrix factorization. *IEEE*, vol. 6, pages 3549–3564, 2018. DOI: 10.1109/access.2017.2788138 48, 68

[3] Léon Bottou. Stochastic gradient learning in neural networks. *Proc. of Neuro-Nimes*, 91(8), 1991. 19, 36, 57

[4] Andrew P. Bradley. The use of the area under the ROC curve in the evaluation of machine learning algorithms. *Pattern Recognition*, vol. 30, pages 1145–1159, Elsevier, 1997. DOI: 10.1016/S0031-3203(96)00142-2 56

[5] Markus Brill, Edith Elkind, Ulle Endriss, and Umberto Grandi. Pairwise diffusion of preference rankings in social networks. In *International Joint Conference on Artificial Intelligence*, pages 130–136, 2016. 81

[6] Da Cao, Liqiang Nie, Xiangnan He, Xiaochi Wei, Shunzhi Zhu, and Tat-Seng Chua. Embedding factorization models for jointly recommending items and user generated lists. In *Proc. of the International ACM SIGIR Conference on Research and Development in Information Retrieval*, pages 585–594, 2017. DOI: 10.1145/3077136.3080779 31, 50, 68

[7] Da Cao, Xiangnan He, Lianhai Miao, Yahui An, Chao Yang, and Richang Hong. Attentive group recommendation. In *Proc. of the International ACM SIGIR Conference on Research and Development in Information Retrieval*, 2018. DOI: 10.1145/3209978.3209998 33

[8] Turgay Celik. Unsupervised change detection in satellite images using principal component analysis and k-means clustering. *IEEE*, vol. 6, pages 772–776, 2009. DOI: 10.1109/lgrs.2009.2025059 59

[9] Chih-Ming Chen, Ming-Feng Tsai, Jen-Yu Liu, and Yi-Hsuan Yang. Using emotional context from article for contextual music recommendation. In *Proc. of the ACM International Conference on Multimedia*, pages 649–652, 2013. DOI: 10.1145/2502081.2502170 65

[10] Jingyuan Chen, Xuemeng Song, Liqiang Nie, Xiang Wang, Hanwang Zhang, and Tat-Seng Chua. Micro tells macro: Predicting the popularity of micro-videos via a transductive model. In *Proc. of the ACM International Conference on Multimedia*, pages 898–907, 2016. DOI: 10.1145/2964284.2964314 18, 70

[11] Jingyuan Chen, Hanwang Zhang, Xiangnan He, Liqiang Nie, Wei Liu, and Tat-Seng Chua. Attentive collaborative filtering: Multimedia recommendation with item- and component-level attention. In *Proc. of the International ACM SIGIR Conference on Research and Development in Information Retrieval*, pages 335–344, 2017. DOI: 10.1145/3077136.3080797 29, 33

[12] Liang-Chieh Chen, George Papandreou, Iasonas Kokkinos, Kevin Murphy, and Alan L. Yuille. DeepLab: Semantic image segmentation with deep convolutional nets, atrous convolution, and fully connected CRFs. *IEEE*, vol. 40, pages 834–848, 2018. DOI: 10.1109/tpami.2017.2699184 67

[13] Long Chen and Yuhang He. Dress fashionably: Learn fashion collocation with deep mixed-category metric learning. In *AAAI Conference on Artificial Intelligence*, pages 2103–2110, 2018. 82

[14] Zhiyong Cheng, Jialie Shen, Lei Zhu, Mohan S. Kankanhalli, and Liqiang Nie. Exploiting music play sequence for music recommendation. In *Proc. of the International Joint Conference on Artificial Intelligence*, pages 3654–3660, 2017. DOI: 10.24963/ijcai.2017/511 37

[15] Zhiyong Cheng, Ying Ding, Lei Zhu, and Mohan S. Kankanhalli. Aspect-aware latent factor model: Rating prediction with ratings and reviews. In *Proc. of the ACM International WWW Conference*, pages 639–648, 2018. DOI: 10.1145/3178876.3186145 37

[16] Yunjey Choi, Minje Choi, Munyoung Kim, Jung-Woo Ha, Sunghun Kim, and Jaegul Choo StarGAN: Unified generative adversarial networks for multi-domain image-to-image translation. In *Proc. of IEEE Conference on Computer Vision and Pattern Recognition*, pages 8789–8797, 2018. DOI: 10.1109/cvpr.2018.00916 101

[17] Lieven De Lathauwer, Bart De Moor, and Joos Vandewalle. A multilinear singular value decomposition. *SIAM*, vol. 21, pages 1253–1278, 2000. DOI: 10.1137/s0895479896305696 48

[18] Yingying Deng, Fan Tang, Weiming Dong, Hanxing Yao, and Bao-Gang Hu. Style-oriented representative paintings selection. In *Special Interest Group on Computer Graphics*, pages 12:1–12:2, 2017. DOI: 10.1145/3145690.3145706 92

[19] Wei Di, Catherine Wah, Anurag Bhardwaj, Robinson Piramuthu, and Neel Sundaresan. Style finder: Fine-grained clothing style detection and retrieval. In *Proc. of the IEEE*

International Conference on Computer Vision and Pattern Recognition Workshops, pages 8–13, 2013. DOI: 10.1109/cvprw.2013.6 25

[20] Aviv Eisenschtat and Lior Wolf. Linking image and text with 2-way nets. *arXiv preprint arXiv:1608.07973*, 2016. DOI: 10.1109/cvpr.2017.201 14

[21] Pedro Felzenszwalb, David McAllester, and Deva Ramanan. A discriminatively trained, multiscale, deformable part model. In *Proc. of the IEEE International Conference on Computer Vision and Pattern Recognition*, pages 1–8, 2008. DOI: 10.1109/cvpr.2008.4587597 13

[22] Fangxiang Feng, Xiaojie Wang, and Ruifan Li. Cross-modal retrieval with correspondence autoencoder. In *Proc. of the ACM International Conference on Multimedia*, pages 7–16, 2014. DOI: 10.1145/2647868.2654902 14

[23] Fuli Feng, Xiangnan He, Yiqun Liu, Liqiang Nie, and Tat-Seng Chua. Learning on partial-order hypergraphs. In *Proc. of the ACM International WWW Conference*, pages 1523–1532, 2018. DOI: 10.1145/3178876.3186064 31

[24] Zunlei Feng, Zhenyun Yu, Yezhou Yang, Yongcheng Jing, Junxiao Jiang, and Mingli Song. Interpretable partitioned embedding for customized multi-item fashion outfit composition. In *Proc. of the International Conference on Multimedia Retrieval*, pages 143–151, ACM, 2018. DOI: 10.1145/3206025.3206048 46, 47, 65, 82

[25] Brendan J. Frey and Delbert Dueck. Clustering by passing messages between data points. *Science*, 315(5814):972–976, 2007. DOI: 10.1126/science.1136800 92

[26] Yue Gao, Meng Wang, Zheng-Jun Zha, Jialie Shen, Xuelong Li, and Xindong Wu. Visual-textual joint relevance learning for tag-based social image search. *IEEE Transactions on Image Processing*, 22(1):363–376, 2013. DOI: 10.1109/tip.2012.2202676 19

[27] Kostadin Georgiev and Preslav Nakov. A non-IID framework for collaborative filtering with restricted Boltzmann machines. In *Proc. of the International Conference on Machine Learning, JMLR.org*, pages 1148–1156, 2013. 14

[28] Xiaoling Gu, Yongkang Wong, Pai Peng, Lidan Shou, Gang Chen, and Mohan S. Kankanhalli. Understanding fashion trends from street photos via neighbor-constrained embedding learning. In *Proc. of the ACM International Conference on Multimedia*, pages 190–198, 2017. DOI: 10.1145/3123266.3123441 65

[29] M. Hadi Kiapour, Xufeng Han, Svetlana Lazebnik, Alexander C. Berg, and Tamara L. Berg. Where to buy it: Matching street clothing photos in online shops. In *Proc. of the IEEE International Conference on Computer Vision*, pages 3343–3351, 2015. DOI: 10.1109/iccv.2015.382 3, 7

[30] Xianjing Han, Xuemeng Song, Jianhua Yin, Yinglong Wang, and Liqiang Nie. Prototype-guided attribute-wise interpretable scheme for clothing matching. In *Proc. of the International ACM SIGIR Conference on Research and Development in Information Retrieval*, pages 785–794, 2019. DOI: 10.1145/3331184.3331245 63

[31] Xintong Han, Zuxuan Wu, Yu-Gang Jiang, and Larry S. Davis. Learning fashion compatibility with bidirectional LSTMs. In *ACM Multimedia Conference on Multimedia Conference*, pages 1078–1086, 2017. DOI: 10.1145/3123266.3123394 9, 28, 47, 57, 65, 71, 79, 82, 86, 89

[32] John A. Hartigan and Manchek A. Wong. Algorithm as 136: A *k*-means clustering algorithm. *JSTOR*, vol. 28, pages 100–108, 1979. DOI: 10.2307/2346830 59

[33] Kaiming He, Xiangyu Zhang, Shaoqing Ren, and Jian Sun. Deep residual learning for image recognition. In *Proc. of the IEEE Conference on Computer Vision and Pattern Recognition*, 2015. DOI: 10.1109/cvpr.2016.90 70

[34] Ruining He and Julian McAuley. VBPR: Visual Bayesian personalized ranking from implicit feedback. In *AAAI Conference on Artificial Intelligence*, pages 144–150, 2016. 14, 66, 68, 72, 81, 83

[35] Ruining He, Chunbin Lin, Jianguo Wang, and Julian McAuley. Sherlock: Sparse hierarchical embeddings for visually-aware one-class collaborative filtering. In *International Joint Conference on Artificial Intelligence*, pages 3740–3746, 2016. 81

[36] Xiangnan He, Hanwang Zhang, Min Yen Kan, and Tat Seng Chua. Fast matrix factorization for online recommendation with implicit feedback. In *Proc. of the International ACM SIGIR Conference on Research and Development in Information Retrieval*, pages 549–558, 2016. DOI: 10.1145/2911451.2911489 31, 48, 50, 60, 65

[37] Xiangnan He, Lizi Liao, Hanwang Zhang, Liqiang Nie, Xia Hu, and Tat-Seng Chua. Neural collaborative filtering. In *Proc. of the ACM International WWW Conference*, pages 173–182, 2017. DOI: 10.1145/3038912.3052569 25, 41, 75

[38] Shintami Chusnul Hidayati, Cheng-Chun Hsu, Yu-Ting Chang, Kai-Lung Hua, Jianlong Fu, and Wen-Huang Cheng. What dress fits me best?: Fashion recommendation on the clothing style for personal body shape. In *ACM Multimedia Conference on Multimedia Conference*, pages 438–446, 2018. DOI: 10.1145/3240508.3240546 79, 82, 92

[39] Geoffrey E. Hinton, Simon Osindero, and Yee-Whye Teh. A fast learning algorithm for deep belief nets. *Neural Computation*, 18(7):1527–1554, 2006. DOI: 10.1162/neco.2006.18.7.1527 14

[40] Geoffrey E. Hinton, Oriol Vinyals, and Jeffrey Dean. Distilling the knowledge in a neural network. *CoRR*, abs/1503.02531, 2015. 29

[41] Wei-Lin Hsiao and Kristen Grauman. Creating capsule wardrobes from fashion images. In *Conference on Computer Vision and Pattern Recognition*, pages 7161–7170, 2018. DOI: 10.1109/cvpr.2018.00748 79, 82, 89

[42] Diane J. Hu, Rob Hall, and Josh Attenberg. Style in the long tail: Discovering unique interests with latent variable models in large scale social e-commerce. In *Proc. of the International ACM SIGKDD Conference*, pages 1640–1649, 2014. DOI: 10.1145/2623330.2623338 13

[43] Yang Hu, Xi Yi, and Larry S. Davis. Collaborative fashion recommendation: A functional tensor factorization approach. In *Proc. of the ACM International Conference on Multimedia*, pages 129–138, 2015. DOI: 10.1145/2733373.2806239 7, 13, 66

[44] Yifan Hu, Yehuda Koren, and Chris Volinsky. Collaborative filtering for implicit feedback datasets. In *International Conference on Data Mining*, pages 263–272, 2008. DOI: 10.1109/icdm.2008.22 81

[45] Zhiting Hu, Xuezhe Ma, Zhengzhong Liu, Eduard H. Hovy, and Eric P. Xing. Harnessing deep neural networks with logic rules. In *Proc. of the Annual Meeting of the Association for Computational Linguistics*, pages 2410–2420, 2016. DOI: 10.18653/v1/p16-1228 28, 29, 31, 32, 33, 70

[46] Zhiting Hu, Zichao Yang, Ruslan Salakhutdinov, and Eric P. Xing. Deep neural networks with massive learned knowledge. In *Proc. of the Conference on Empirical Methods in Natural Language Processing*, pages 1670–1679, The Association for Computational Linguistics, 2016. DOI: 10.18653/v1/d16-1173 32

[47] Phillip Isola, Jun-Yan Zhu, Tinghui Zhou, and Alexei A. Efros. Image-to-image translation with conditional adversarial networks. In *Proc. of IEEE Conference on Computer Vision and Pattern Recognition*, pages 1125–1134, 2017. DOI: 10.1109/cvpr.2017.632 101

[48] Tomoharu Iwata, Shinji Wanatabe, and Hiroshi Sawada. Fashion coordinates recommender system using photographs from fashion magazines. In *Proc. of the International Joint Conference on Artificial Intelligence*, vol. 22, page 2262, AAAI, 2011. DOI: 10.5591/978-1-57735-516-8/IJCAI11-377 13

[49] Vignesh Jagadeesh, Robinson Piramuthu, Anurag Bhardwaj, Wei Di, and Neel Sundaresan. Large scale visual recommendations from street fashion images. In *Proc. of the International ACM SIGKDD Conference*, pages 1925–1934, 2014. DOI: 10.1145/2623330.2623332 3, 7

[50] Rong-rong Ji, Xing Xie, Hongxun Yao, and Wei-Ying Ma. Mining city landmarks from blogs by graph modeling. In *Proc. of the ACM International Conference on Multimedia*, pages 105–114, 2009. DOI: 10.1145/1631272.1631289 19

[51] Yangqing Jia, Evan Shelhamer, Jeff Donahue, Sergey Karayev, Jonathan Long, Ross Girshick, Sergio Guadarrama, and Trevor Darrell. Caffe: Convolutional architecture for fast feature embedding. In *Proc. of the ACM International Conference on Multimedia*, pages 675–678, 2014. DOI: 10.1145/2647868.2654889 18, 36

[52] Lu Jiang, Shoou-I Yu, Deyu Meng, Yi Yang, Teruko Mitamura, and Alexander G. Hauptmann. Fast and accurate content-based semantic search in 100 m internet videos. In *Proc. of the ACM International Conference on Multimedia*, pages 49–58, 2015. DOI: 10.1145/2733373.2806237 25, 41, 61, 76

[53] Shuhui Jiang, Yue Wu, and Yun Fu. Deep bi-directional cross-triplet embedding for cross-domain clothing retrieval. In *ACM Conference on Multimedia Conference*, pages 52–56, 2016. DOI: 10.1145/2964284.2967182 88

[54] Wang-Cheng Kang, Chen Fang, Zhaowen Wang, and Julian McAuley. Visually-aware fashion recommendation and design with generative image models. In *IEEE International Conference on Data Mining*, pages 207–216, 2017. DOI: 10.1109/icdm.2017.30 79

[55] Aditya Khosla, Atish Das Sarma, and Raffay Hamid. What makes an image popular? In *Proc. of the ACM International WWW Conference*, pages 867–876, 2014. DOI: 10.1145/2566486.2567996 18, 70

[56] Donghyun Kim, Chanyoung Park, Jinoh Oh, Sungyoung Lee, and Hwanjo Yu. Convolutional matrix factorization for document context-aware recommendation. In *Proc. of the ACM Conference on Recommender Systems*, pages 233–240, 2016. DOI: 10.1145/2959100.2959165 48, 68

[57] Yoon Kim. Convolutional neural networks for sentence classification. In *Proc. of the Conference on Empirical Methods in Natural Language Processing*, pages 1746–1751, 2014. DOI: 10.3115/v1/d14-1181 36, 70

[58] Diederik P. Kingma and Jimmy Ba. Adam: A method for stochastic optimization. *ArXiv Preprint ArXiv:1412.6980*, 2014. 71

[59] Yehuda Koren. Factorization meets the neighborhood: A multifaceted collaborative filtering model. In *Proc. of the International ACM SIGKDD Conference*, pages 426–434, 2008. DOI: 10.1145/1401890.1401944 25

[60] Yehuda Koren and Robert Bell. Advances in collaborative filtering. *Recommender Systems Handbook*, pages 77–118, 2015. DOI: 10.1007/978-1-4899-7637-6_3 68

[61] Yehuda Koren, Robert Bell, and Chris Volinsky. Matrix factorization techniques for recommender systems. *IEEE Computer*, vol. 42, no. 8, pages 30–37, 2009. DOI: 10.1109/mc.2009.263 48

[62] Alex Krizhevsky, Ilya Sutskever, and Geoffrey E. Hinton. Imagenet classification with deep convolutional neural networks. In *Proc. of the Advances in Neural Information Processing Systems*, pages 1097–1105, 2012. DOI: 10.1145/3065386 14, 55

[63] Ranjitha Kumar and Kristen Vaccaro. An experimentation engine for data-driven fashion systems. In *AAAI Spring Symposium Series*, 2017. 79

[64] Yann LeCun, Yoshua Bengio, and Geoffrey Hinton. Deep learning. *Nature*, 521(7553):436–444, 2015. DOI: 10.1038/nature14539 14

[65] Daniel D. Lee and H. Sebastian Seung. Learning the parts of objects by non-negative matrix factorization. *Nature Publishing Group*, vol. 401, page 788, 1999. DOI: 10.1038/44565 46, 48

[66] Xuelong Li, Guosheng Cui, and Yongsheng Dong. Graph regularized non-negative low-rank matrix factorization for image clustering. *IEEE*, vol. 47, pages 3840–3853, 2017. DOI: 10.1109/tcyb.2016.2585355 51

[67] Yuncheng Li, Liangliang Cao, Jiang Zhu, and Jiebo Luo. Mining fashion outfit composition using an end-to-end deep learning approach on set data. *IEEE Transactions on Multimedia*, 19(8):1946–1955, 2017. DOI: 10.1109/tmm.2017.2690144 13, 14, 28, 47, 65, 82

[68] Jian Han Lim, Nurul Japar, Chun Chet Ng, and Chee Seng Chan. Unprecedented usage of pre-trained CNNs on beauty product. In *Proc. of the ACM International Conference on Multimedia*, pages 2068–2072, 2018. DOI: 10.1145/3240508.3266433 70

[69] Yujie Lin, Pengjie Ren, Zhumin Chen, Zhaochun Ren, Jun Ma, and Maarten de Rijke. Explainable fashion recommendation with joint outfit matching and comment generation. *IEEE Transactions on Knowledge and Data Engineering*, 2018. DOI: 10.1109/tkde.2019.2906190 47

[70] Yujie Lin, Pengjie Ren, Zhumin Chen, Zhaochun Ren, Jun Ma, and Maarten de Rijke. Improving outfit recommendation with co-supervision of fashion generation. In *International World Wide Web Conference*, 2019. DOI: 10.1145/3308558.3313614 82

[71] Jingyuan Liu and Hong Lu. Deep fashion analysis with feature map upsampling and landmark-driven attention. In *European Conference on Computer Vision Workshops*, pages 30–36, 2018. DOI: 10.1007/978-3-030-11015-4_4 82

[72] Meng Liu, Liqiang Nie, Meng Wang, and Baoquan Chen. Towards micro-video understanding by joint sequential-sparse modeling. In *Proc. of the ACM International Conference on Multimedia*, pages 970–978, 2017. DOI: 10.1145/3123266.3123341 70

[73] Meng Liu, Xiang Wang, Liqiang Nie, Xiangnan He, Baoquan Chen, and Tat-Seng Chua. Attentive moment retrieval in videos. In *Proc. of the International ACM SIGIR Conference on Research and Development in Information Retrieval*, pages 15–24, 2018. DOI: 10.1145/3209978.3210003 50

[74] Meng Liu, Xiang Wang, Liqiang Nie, Qi Tian, Baoquan Chen, and Tat-Seng Chua. Cross-modal moment localization in videos. In *Proc. of the ACM International Conference on Multimedia*, pages 843–851, 2018. DOI: 10.1145/3240508.3240549 67

[75] Meng Liu, Liqiang Nie, Xiang Wang, Qi Tian, and Baoquan Chen. Online data organizer: Micro-video categorization by structure-guided multimodal dictionary learning. *IEEE*, vol. 28, pages 1235–1247, 2019. DOI: 10.1109/tip.2018.2875363 50

[76] Si Liu, Jiashi Feng, Zheng Song, Tianzhu Zhang, Hanqing Lu, Changsheng Xu, and Shuicheng Yan. Hi, magic closet, tell me what to wear! In *Proc. of the ACM International Conference on Multimedia*, pages 619–628, 2012. DOI: 10.1145/2393347.2393433 3, 7, 13

[77] Si Liu, Zheng Song, Guangcan Liu, Changsheng Xu, Hanqing Lu, and Shuicheng Yan. Street-to-shop: Cross-scenario clothing retrieval via parts alignment and auxiliary set. In *Proc. of the IEEE International Conference on Computer Vision and Pattern Recognition*, pages 3330–3337, 2012. DOI: 10.1109/cvpr.2012.6248071 13

[78] Siyuan Liu, Qiong Wu, and Chunyan Miao. Personalized recommendation considering secondary implicit feedback. In *Proc. of the IEEE International Conference on Agents*, pages 87–92, 2018. DOI: 10.1109/agents.2018.8460053 68

[79] Xin Liu, An Li, Ji-Xiang Du, Shu-Juan Peng, and Wentao Fan. Efficient cross-modal retrieval via flexible supervised collective matrix factorization hashing, *Multimedia Tools and Applications*, vol. 77, no. 21, pages 28665–28683, Springer, 2018. DOI: 10.1007/s11042-018-6006-5 48

[80] Ziwei Liu, Ping Luo, Shi Qiu, Xiaogang Wang, and Xiaoou Tang. Deepfashion: Powering robust clothes recognition and retrieval with rich annotations. In *IEEE Conference on Computer Vision and Pattern Recognition*, pages 1096–1104, 2016. DOI: 10.1109/cvpr.2016.124 88

[81] Ziwei Liu, Ping Luo, Shi Qiu, Xiaogang Wang, and Xiaoou Tang. Deepfashion: Powering robust clothes recognition and retrieval with rich annotations. In *Proc. of IEEE*

Conference on Computer Vision and Pattern Recognition, pages 1096–1104, 2016. DOI: 10.1109/cvpr.2016.124 55

[82] Babak Loni, Roberto Pagano, Martha Larson, and Alan Hanjalic. Bayesian personalized ranking with multi-channel user feedback. In *Proc. of the ACM Conference on Recommender Systems*, pages 361–364, 2016. DOI: 10.1145/2959100.2959163 68

[83] Maryam Ziaeefard, Jaime Camacaro, and Carolina Bessega. Hierarchical feature map characterization in fashion interpretation. In *Conference on Computer and Robot Vision*, pages 88–94, 2018. DOI: 10.1109/crv.2018.00022 82

[84] Yihui Ma, Jia Jia, Suping Zhou, Jingtian Fu, Yejun Liu, and Zijian Tong. Towards better understanding the clothing fashion styles: A multimodal deep learning approach. In *Proc. of the International Joint Conference on Artificial Intelligence*, pages 38–44, AAAI Press, 2017. 34

[85] Laurens van der Maaten and Geoffrey Hinton. Visualizing data using t-SNE. *Journal of Machine Learning Research*, 9:2579–2605, 2008. 92

[86] Julian McAuley, Christopher Targett, Qinfeng Shi, and Anton Van Den Hengel. Image-based recommendations on styles and substitutes. In *Proc. of the International ACM SI-GIR Conference on Research and Development in Information Retrieval*, pages 43–52, 2015. DOI: 10.1145/2766462.2767755 7, 13, 21, 28, 37, 47, 57

[87] Julian J. McAuley, Christopher Targett, Qinfeng Shi, and Anton van den Hengel. Image-based recommendations on styles and substitutes. In *ACM SIGIR Conference on Research and Development in Information Retrieval*, pages 43–52, 2015. DOI: 10.1145/2766462.2767755 9, 82

[88] Mehdi Mirza and Simon Osindero. Conditional generative adversarial nets. *arXiv preprint arXiv:1411.1784*, 2014. 101

[89] Andriy Mnih and Ruslan R. Salakhutdinov. Probabilistic matrix factorization. In *Advances in Neural Information Processing Systems*, pages 1257–1264, 2008. 48

[90] Jiquan Ngiam, Aditya Khosla, Mingyu Kim, Juhan Nam, Honglak Lee, and Andrew Y. Ng. Multimodal deep learning. In *Proc. of the International Conference on Machine Learning*, pages 689–696, JMLR.org, 2011. 14

[91] Liqiang Nie, Xuemeng Song, and Tat-Seng Chua. *Learning from Multiple Social Networks*. Synthesis Lectures on Information Concepts, Retrieval, and Services. Morgan & Claypool Publishers, 2016. DOI: 10.2200/s00714ed1v01y201603icr048 81

[92] Charles Packer, Julian McAuley, and Arnau Ramisa. Visually-aware personalized recommendation using interpretable image representations, *ArXiv Preprint ArXiv:1806.09820*, 2018. 68

[93] Rong Pan, Yunhong Zhou, Bin Cao, Nathan Nan Liu, Rajan M. Lukose, Martin Scholz, and Qiang Yang. One-class collaborative filtering. In *International Conference on Data Mining*, pages 502–511, 2008. DOI: 10.1109/icdm.2008.16 81

[94] Xueming Qian, He Feng, Guoshuai Zhao, and Tao Mei. Personalized recommendation combining user interest and social circle. *IEEE Transactions on Knowledge and Data Engineering*, 26(7):1763–1777, 2014. DOI: 10.1109/tkde.2013.168 12, 21, 37

[95] Meng Qu, Jian Tang, Jingbo Shang, Xiang Ren, Ming Zhang, and Jiawei Han. An attention-based collaboration framework for multi-view network representation learning. In *Proc. of the ACM International Conference on Information and Knowledge Management*, pages 1767–1776, 2017. DOI: 10.1145/3132847.3133021 33

[96] Alec Radford, Luke Metz, and Soumith Chintala. Unsupervised representation learning with deep convolutional generative adversarial networks. *International Conference on Learning Representations*, *ArXiv Preprint ArXiv:1511.06434*, 2016. 101

[97] Dimitrios Rafailidis and Fabio Crestani. Cluster-based joint matrix factorization hashing for cross-modal retrieval. In *Proc. of the International ACM SIGIR Conference on Research and Development in Information Retrieval*, pages 781–784, 2016. DOI: 10.1145/2911451.2914710 48

[98] Janarthanan Rajendran, Mitesh M. Khapra, Sarath Chandar, and Balaraman Ravindran. Bridge correlational neural networks for multilingual multimodal representation learning. *arXiv preprint arXiv:1510.03519*, 2015. DOI: 10.18653/v1/n16-1021 14, 30

[99] Steffen Rendle and Lars Schmidt-Thieme. Pairwise interaction tensor factorization for personalized tag recommendation. In *Proc. of the ACM International WSDM Conference*, pages 81–90, 2010. DOI: 10.1145/1718487.1718498 19, 57

[100] Steffen Rendle, Christoph Freudenthaler, Zeno Gantner, and Lars Schmidt-Thieme. BPR: Bayesian personalized ranking from implicit feedback. In *Proc. of the International Conference on Uncertainty in Artificial Intelligence*, pages 452–461, AUAI Press, 2009. 12, 17, 28, 31, 47, 50, 64, 68, 71, 81, 84

[101] Hosnieh Sattar, Gerard Pons-Moll, and Mario Fritz. Fashion is taking shape: Understanding clothing preference based on body shape from online sources. In *IEEE Winter Conference on Applications of Computer Vision*, pages 968–977, 2019. DOI: 10.1109/wacv.2019.00108 79, 82

[102] Aliaksei Severyn and Alessandro Moschitti. Twitter sentiment analysis with deep convolutional neural networks. In *Proc. of the International ACM SIGIR Conference on Research and Development in Information Retrieval*, pages 959–962, 2015. DOI: 10.1145/2766462.2767830 36, 70

[103] Hiroyuki Shinnou, Masayuki Asahara, K. Komiya, and M. Sasaki. NWJC2Vec: Word embedding data constructed from NINJAL Web Japanese Corpus, *Journal of Natural Language Processing*, (in Japanese), vol. 24, pages 705–720, 2017. DOI: 10.5715/jnlp.24.705 70

[104] Edgar Simo-Serra, Sanja Fidler, Francesc Moreno-Noguer, and Raquel Urtasun. Neuroaesthetics in fashion: Modeling the perception of fashionability. In *Proc. of the IEEE International Conference on Computer Vision and Pattern Recognition*, pages 869–877, 2015. DOI: 10.1109/cvpr.2015.7298688 13

[105] Karen Simonyan and Andrew Zisserman. Very deep convolutional networks for large-scale image recognition. In *International Conference on Learning Representations*, 2015. 88

[106] Xuemeng Song, Liqiang Nie, Luming Zhang, Mohammad Akbari, and Tat-Seng Chua. Multiple social network learning and its application in volunteerism tendency prediction. In *Proc. of the International ACM SIGIR Conference on Research and Development in Information Retrieval*, pages 213–222, 2015. DOI: 10.1145/2766462.2767726 36, 70

[107] Xuemeng Song, Liqiang Nie, Luming Zhang, Maofu Liu, and Tat-Seng Chua. Interest inference via structure-constrained multi-source multi-task learning. In *Proc. of the International Joint Conference on Artificial Intelligence*, pages 2371–2377, AAAI Press, 2015. 36, 70

[108] Xuemeng Song, Fuli Feng, Jinhuan Liu, Zekun Li, Liqiang Nie, and Jun Ma. Neurostylist: Neural compatibility modeling for clothing matching. In *ACM Multimedia Conference or Multimedia Conference*, pages 753–761, 2017. DOI: 10.1145/3123266.3123314 28, 29, 37, 47, 57, 65, 67, 71, 82, 84

[109] Xuemeng Song, Fuli Feng, Xianjing Han, Xin Yang, Wei Liu, and Liqiang Nie. Neural compatibility modeling with attentive knowledge distillation. In *Proc. of the International ACM SIGIR Conference on Research and Development in Information Retrieval*, pages 5–14, 2018. DOI: 10.1145/3209978.3209996 50, 65, 82

[110] Guang Lu Sun, Zhi Qi Cheng, Xiao Wu, and Qiang Peng. Personalized clothing recommendation combining user social circle and fashion style consistency, *Multimedia Tools and Applications*, vol. 77, pages 1–24, 2017. DOI: 10.1007/s11042-017-5245-1 66

[111] Yifan Sun, Liang Zheng, Weijian Deng, and Shengjin Wang. SVDNet for pedestrian retrieval. In *Proc. of the IEEE International Conference on Computer Vision*, pages 3800–3808, 2017. DOI: 10.1109/iccv.2017.410 48

[112] Hossein Talebi and Peyman Milanfar. NIMA: Neural image assessment. *IEEE Transactions on Image Processing*, 27(8):998–4011, 2018. DOI: 10.1109/tip.2018.2831899 89

[113] Jun Tang, Ke Wang, and Ling Shao. Supervised matrix factorization hashing for cross-modal retrieval, *IEEE Transactions on Image Processing*, vol. 25, pages 3157–3166, 2016. DOI: 10.1109/tip.2016.2564638 48

[114] Thanh Tran, Kyumin Lee, Yiming Liao, and Dongwon Lee. Regularizing matrix factorization with user and item embeddings for recommendation. In *Proc. of the ACM International Conference on Information and Knowledge Management*, pages 687–696, 2018. DOI: 10.1145/3269206.3271730 48, 65

[115] Mariya I. Vasileva, Bryan A. Plummer, Krishna Dusad, Shreya Rajpal, Ranjitha Kumar, and David A. Forsyth. Learning type-aware embeddings for fashion compatibility. In *European Conference on Computer Vision*, pages 405–421, 2018. DOI: 10.1007/978-3-030-01270-0_24 82

[116] Andreas Veit, Balazs Kovacs, Sean Bell, Julian McAuley, Kavita Bala, and Serge J. Belongie. Learning visual clothing style with heterogeneous dyadic co-occurrences. In *IEEE International Conference on Computer Vision*, pages 4642–4650, 2015. DOI: 10.1109/iccv.2015.527 82

[117] Daixin Wang, Peng Cui, Mingdong Ou, and Wenwu Zhu. Deep multimodal hashing with orthogonal regularization. In *Proc. of the International Joint Conference on Artificial Intelligence*, pages 2291–2297, AAAI Press, 2015. 14

[118] Daixin Wang, Peng Cui, and Wenwu Zhu. Structural deep network embedding. In *Proc. of the International ACM SIGKDD Conference*, pages 1225–1234, 2016. DOI: 10.1145/2939672.2939753 14, 15

[119] Wenguan Wang, Yuanlu Xu, Jianbing Shen, and Song-Chun Zhu. Attentive fashion grammar network for fashion landmark detection and clothing category classification. In *Conference on Computer Vision and Pattern Recognition*, pages 4271–4280, 2018. DOI: 10.1109/cvpr.2018.00449 82

[120] Xiang Wang, Xiangnan He, Yixin Cao, Meng Liu, and Tat-Seng Chua. KGAT: Knowledge graph attention network for recommendation. In *Proc. of the International ACM SIGKDD Conference on Knowledge Discovery and Data Mining*, 2019. DOI: 10.1145/3292500.3330989 50

[121] Xiang Wang, Xiangnan He, Meng Wang, Fuli Feng, and Tat-Seng Chua. Neural graph collaborative filtering. In *Proc. of the International ACM SIGIR Conference on Research and Development in Informaion Retrieval*, 2019. DOI: 10.1145/3331184.3331267 48

[122] Xinxi Wang and Ye Wang. Improving content-based and hybrid music recommendation using deep learning. In *Proc. of the ACM International Conference on Multimedia*, pages 627–636, 2014. DOI: 10.1145/2647868.2654940 12, 21, 37

[123] Zheng Wang, Xiang Bai, Mang Ye, and Shin'ichi Satoh. Incremental deep hidden attribute learning. In *Proc. of the ACM International Conference on Multimedia*, pages 72–80. ACM, 2018. DOI: 10.1145/3240508.3240510 67

[124] Wei Xu, Xin Liu, and Yihong Gong. Document clustering based on non-negative matrix factorization. In *Proc. of the International ACM SIGIR Conference on Research and Development in Information Retrieval*, pages 267–273, 2003. DOI: 10.1145/860435.860485 48

[125] Kota Yamaguchi, M. Hadi Kiapour, Luis E. Ortiz, and Tamara L. Berg. Parsing clothing in fashion photographs. In *Proc. of the IEEE International Conference on Computer Vision and Pattern Recognition*, pages 3570–3577, 2012. DOI: 10.1109/cvpr.2012.6248101 7

[126] Kota Yamaguchi, M. Hadi Kiapour, Luis E. Ortiz, and Tamara L. Berg. Retrieving similar styles to parse clothing. *IEEE Transactions on Pattern Analysis and Machine Intelligence*, 37(5):1028–1040, 2015. DOI: 10.1109/tpami.2014.2353624 7

[127] Xun Yang, Yunshan Ma, Lizi Liao, Meng Wang, and Tat-Seng Chua. TransNFCM: Translation-based neural fashion compatibility modeling. In *AAAI Conference on Artificial Intelligence*, pages 403–410, 2019. 65, 82

[128] Jiangchao Yao, Yanfeng Wang, Ya Zhang, Jun Sun, and Jun Zhou. Joint latent Dirichlet allocation for social tags, *IEEE Transactions on Multimedia*, vol. 20, pages 224–237, 2018. DOI: 10.1109/TMM.2017.2716829 76

[129] Hongzhi Yin, Hongxu Chen, Xiaoshuai Sun, Hao Wang, Yang Wang, and Quoc Viet Hung Nguyen. SPTF: A scalable probabilistic tensor factorization model for semantic-aware behavior prediction. In *Proc. of the IEEE International Conference on Data Mining*, pages 585–594, 2017. DOI: 10.1109/icdm.2017.68 41, 61, 76

[130] Hongzhi Yin, Weiqing Wang, Hao Wang, Ling Chen, and Xiaofang Zhou. Spatial-aware hierarchical collaborative deep learning for POI recommendation, *IEEE Transactions on Knowledge and Data Engineering*, vol. 29, pages 2537–2551, 2017. DOI: 10.1109/tkde.2017.2741484 29

[131] Ruichi Yu, Ang Li, Vlad I. Morariu, and Larry S. Davis. Visual relationship detection with internal and external linguistic knowledge distillation. In *Proc. of the IEEE International Conference on Computer Vision*, pages 1974–1982, IEEE Computer Society, 2017. DOI: 10.1109/iccv.2017.121 29, 30

[132] Wenhui Yu, Huidi Zhang, Xiangnan He, Xu Chen, Li Xiong, and Zheng Qin. Aesthetic-based clothing recommendation. In *Proc. of World Wide Web Conference on World Wide Web*, pages 649–658, 2018. DOI: 10.1145/3178876.3186146 82, 89

[133] Hanwang Zhang, Zheng-Jun Zha, Yang Yang, Shuicheng Yan, Yue Gao, and Tat-Seng Chua Attribute-augmented semantic hierarchy: Towards bridging semantic gap and intention gap in image retrieval. In *Proc. of the ACM International Conference on Multimedia*, pages 33–42, 2013. DOI: 10.1145/2502081.2502093 36, 57, 71

[134] Hanwang Zhang, Xindi Shang, Wenzhuo Yang, Huan Xu, Huanbo Luan, and Tat-Seng Chua Online collaborative learning for open-vocabulary visual classifiers. In *Proc. of the IEEE Conference on Computer Vision and Pattern Recognition*, pages 2809–2817, 2016. DOI: 10.1109/cvpr.2016.307 18

[135] Hanwang Zhang, Zawlin Kyaw, Shih-Fu Chang, and Tat-Seng Chua. Visual translation embedding network for visual relation detection. In *IEEE Conference on Computer Vision and Pattern Recognition*, pages 3107–3115, 2017. DOI: 10.1109/cvpr.2017.331 41, 61

[136] Xishan Zhang, Jia Jia, Ke Gao, Yongdong Zhang, Dongming Zhang, Jintao Li, and Qi Tian. Trip outfits advisor: Location-oriented clothing recommendation. *IEEE Transactions on Multimedia*, 19(11):2533–2544, 2017. DOI: 10.1109/tmm.2017.2696825 88

[137] Zhengzhong Zhou, Xiu Di, Wei Zhou, and Liqing Zhang. Fashion sensitive clothing recommendation using hierarchical collocation model. In *ACM Multimedia Conference on Multimedia Conference*, pages 1119–1127, 2018. DOI: 10.1145/3240508.3240596 82

[138] Jun-Yan Zhu, Taesung Park, Phillip Isola, and Alexei A. Efros. Unpaired image-to-image translation using cycle-consistent adversarial networks. In *International Conference on Computer Vision*, pages 2223–2232, 2017. DOI: 10.1109/iccv.2017.244 101

[139] Al-Halah Ziad, Stiefelhagen Rainer, and Grauman Kristen. Fashion forward: Forecasting visual style in fashion. In *Proc. of the IEEE International Conference on Computer Vision*, pages 388–397, 2017. DOI: 10.1109/iccv.2017.50 48, 49

Authors' Biographies

XUEMENG SONG

Xuemeng Song received a B.E. from the University of Science and Technology of China in 2012, and a Ph.D. from the School of Computing, National University of Singapore in 2016. She is currently an assistant professor of Shandong University, Jinan, China. Her research interests include information retrieval and social network analysis. She has published several papers in top venues, such as ACM SIGIR, MM, TIP, and TOIS. In addition, she has served as a reviewer for many top conferences and journals.

LIQIANG NIE

Liqiang Nie is currently a professor with the School of Computer Science and Technology, Shandong University. In addition, he is the adjunct dean with the Shandong AI institute. He received his B.Eng. and Ph.D. from Xi'an Jiaotong University in 2009 and the National University of Singapore (NUS) in 2013, respectively. After his Ph.D., Dr. Nie continued his research at NUS as a research follow for three and a half years. His research interests lie primarily in multimedia computing and information retrieval. Dr. Nie has authored and co-authored more than 100 papers for SIGIR, ACM MM, TOIS, and TIP, and received more than 4400 Google Scholar citations. He is an AE of Information Science, and an area chair of ACM MM 2018/2019.

YINGLONG WANG

Yinglong Wang is a researcher, Ph.D. Supervisor, and Party Secretary of the Qilu University of Technology (Shandong Academy of Sciences). He was declared a Young and Middle-aged Expert with outstanding contributions to Shandong Province and High-End Think Tank Expert of Shandong Province, and he enjoys special government allowances from the State Council. He serves as the vice chairman of the Shandong Science and Technology Association, the president of the Shandong Internet of Things Association, the director of the China-Australia International Health Technology Joint Laboratory, a member of the Shandong Informatization Expert Group, a member of the Shandong Informatization Expert Advisory Committee, and the deputy chairman of the Shandong Information Standardization Technical Committee. Dr. Wang's main research areas are medical artificial intelligence and high-performance computing. In recent years, he has taken charge of more than 20 national, provincial, and ministerial projects. The scientific research projects led by him won 2 first, 4 second, and 2 third prizes at the Shandong Science and Technology Progress Awards. He has published more than 60 top academic papers and owns more than 20 authorized invention patents. Moreover, he organized the compilation of three volumes of national standards.